THE
HANDBOOK
OF SMALL
BUSINESS

THE
HANDBOOK
OF SMALL
BUSINESS

DICK BAYNTON

Rev. date: 02/09/2016

To order additional copies of this book, contact:
Xlibris
1-888-795-4274
www.Xlibris.com
Orders@Xlibris.com
733004

CONTENTS

To my family, especially to my late wife, Virginia Elaine Hubbard Baynton, whose name I was fortunate enough to draw in the greatest lottery of all, lifetime partnership.

Foreword

The four legs of the operating stool of any business are:

Productivity can be measured in many different ways and can always be improved. Maintain all tools, equipment, and vehicles to avoid downtime. Machines respond to fast, accurate operation. Your employees should be the most competent and efficient available. Veto Murphy's Law. (Work increases to fill the time available.)

Quality is not optional. Leave mediocrity to others (especially competitors).

Safety is a repetitive discipline on the part of every person in the company. Accidents are costly beyond measure.

Attitude reflects the satisfaction of working toward goals and achieving them as individuals, as departments, and as members of a highly successful company.

Note: All are equal in importance, and all four legs must be executed; three out of four is not good enough!

Preface

Starting a business is like operating an engine; they both need constant attention and maintenance to run smoothly.

When you are planning to start a business, here are some guidelines to follow for long-term success:

1. Develop a vision of what you want your company to be and where you want it to go.
2. Create and publicize your company mission statement.
3. Produce a business plan annually for at least one year ahead. Because the economy shifts so quickly, make sure that your business plans have built-in flexibility.
4. Focus on the bottom line—not the top line; growth is the reward for careful planning.
5. Forge partnerships with employees, customers, suppliers, and capital sources.
6. Communicate plans and ideas to all employee partners.
7. Hire and keep outstanding people.
8. Insist on safety in everything; live it, love it, train for it.
9. Develop and maintain individual, departmental, and company productivity.
10. Maintain highest quality; transcend all competition.
11. Empower employee partners; they will help achieve lofty goals.
12. Exercise leadership; people respect and often emulate great leaders.
13. Evaluate all activities; gather and use feedback.
14. Seek, develop, and manage market niches carefully.
15. Sell long-term value; it is permanent. Price is temporary.
16. Produce more than you promise.
17. Curry repeat customers, for they are the lifeblood of your enterprise.

Acknowledgments

The concepts and statements presented in this manual come from both classroom education as well as the "school of hard knocks." Information comes from corporate training—the operation of functions and human resources in corporate management, the operation of successful entrepreneurial businesses, and the learning from mistakes from all the challenges mentioned.

In addition, strategic planning, operation, and follow-up have been sharpened by attendance at seminars and reading the many theories, thoughts, and ideas of leading business authors, advisors, and consultants.

My knowledge has been enhanced by the consultancy services that have been rendered to a broad list of business leaders who have solicited and received my advice and counsel. Their challenges became mine, allowing all participants the ability to develop solutions by thinking "outside the box."

While there are many sources of information and inspiration from speeches, presentations, seminars, books, professors, consultants, and others in this book, all thoughts, written and spoken, have been distilled into the author's words, phrasing, and paragraphs.

Introduction

Where there is liberty and freedom, there is often a predisposition for many citizens to become entrepreneurs, business owners. Often, as former employees of other enterprises, these ambitious people bet their skills and their sometimes-scarce resources against fairly high odds that a profitable living can be generated while serving customers.

The U.S. Census Bureau reports that There were 27.6 million active businesses as of 2012. According to the report, 9.9 million businesses were owned by women or about 36 percent of all enterprises. Past records kept by the U.S. Census Bureau of the U.S. Department of Commerce indicate that about 11 percent to 12 percent of the total number (approximately 3.5 million) businesses are "born," and about the same number "die" each year. These statistics suggest that forming a new business is fairly high risk and requires vast knowledge, hard work, and focus on the varied issues that accompany leadership and operation of a going concern.

In order to achieve success in business, owners and managers must navigate the rough waters of initial and continuing capitalization, competition, taxes, employee productivity, product and service obsolescence, and a host of other obstacles and opportunities. The result must be customer satisfaction followed by profit,* usually accompanied by a strategy that is the outgrowth of a challenging but reasonable business plan, inspired leadership, and productive employees. Associated with these conditions, there must be broad increasing demand for the company's products and services at value pricing as perceived by prospects and customers.

You will not become rich or successful or famous simply by reading this book. However, the ideas offered in these pages should ignite thoughts and actions of creativity that set your company above the competition. Over the years of

---

* If your organization is nonprofit by plan and design, profit usually takes shape as reinvestment of incremental cash in assets, people, and services that amplify customer satisfaction and growth.

successful operation, owners will need to consider a succession plan that provides the best and most rewarding outcome for those that have worked so diligently to achieve success. Keep this handbook nearby and refer to it frequently to remind you of some of the actions that can be taken to insure success.

Problems will become challenges, challenges will become opportunities, and opportunities will become realities. Good luck in your quest for success in the business of your choice!

Chapter 1

ACCIDENTS

Accidents are expensive and often long-lasting; teach safety, learn safety, live safety.

Be sure to report all *lost time* accidents to your insurance company and to authorities as required by law. Accidents involving bones, joints, muscles, internal organs, neck, and head injuries should be reported and treated by medical professionals. Do not try to save time and money by amateur diagnoses and treatments.

Treat all persons with respect, and make sure all injuries are attended to professionally and quickly. Review the reasons for the accident occurrence, and take steps to avoid recurrence of accidents by anyone in the company. Accident-prone workers should always be assigned to jobs that are extremely low risk. Careless high-risk workers should work elsewhere.

Make sure safety devices appropriate to your company are perpetually available for immediate use. Items such as safety goggles (glasses), ear protection, breathing apparatus, eye-wash founts, first-aid kits, and even heart defibrillators are useful items to have ready in case of emergency. It may be helpful to hold training classes for emergency heart failure (CPR).

Engage your insurance agent to conduct periodic safety classes or clinics.

Annual safety celebrations and recognition will help keep safety at the forefront with all employees.

Chapter 2

ACCOUNTANTS

*Victories are achieved not by cleverness and wile but by focusing on
the goal with unrelenting persistence until the objective is achieved.*

Selection of an accountant to do tax calculations and filings for all your taxes is crucial. Here are some guidelines:

Make sure your outside accountant is highly qualified and experienced. There are many fine accountants that are not licensed CPAs, but recipients of this designation have completed several years of work and passed rigid tests of capability. Even when your accountant is not a licensed CPA, it is often a good idea to have a review by a CPA at year-end and engage either a CPA or enrolled agent to compute your tax liability.

Be sure your accountant/auditor has an almost perfect record of on-time performance meeting tax deadlines and other important dates. Likewise, make sure your in-house accountant or bookkeeper provides all necessary data to the outside firm in a timely manner.

Have fee schedules for the work you plan to have your accountant perform. This is needed for budgeting and control.

Get guidance from your accountant or taxing authorities on the rules for specific taxes and fees and due dates payable to city, county, state, and federal authorities.

Be honest to a fault with all discussions with your bookkeeper and accountant/ auditor. Honesty and accuracy are the earmarks of a successful enterprise.

Produce balance sheets and profit and loss statements monthly. Count inventory frequently for accuracy.

Make sure all your taxes are paid on time and that all possible legal deductions have been taken.

If you feel you and your company are not receiving fair treatment from any taxing authority, speak to a supervisor. Keep talking to supervisors until you get the person who can and does provide appropriate responses. If you never get to that supervisor, you may need an attorney or professional specialist.

Chapter 3

ACCOUNTS PAYABLE

Take care of suppliers, and they will take care of you.

Accounts payable are a total of all purchases payable within the vendors' policies of their current receivables, terms of payment, and receipt and delinquency. Many suppliers offer cash discounts for payment within certain time spans between invoicing or delivery and customer payment. Great savings can be made by keeping supplier accounts current. For example, a company that purchases $1,000 per month or $12,000 per year can save $20 per month or $240 each year by "discounting" their purchases if the supplier offers a 2 percent discount when payment is made within terms, usually from ten to thirty days.

On the other hand, if payment is not made within terms, the savings lost (lost opportunity) is $240. Consider that by not taking discounts, you forego payments to other suppliers or liquidation of short-term or long-term debt.

Cost savings can also accrue by quantity purchasing where a discount of 5 percent might be available for buying one thousand units of a needed product instead of five hundred. As your company grows, the opportunity for savings by taking purchase discounts in quantity and timely payments adds up to substantial amounts that can be used for important alternative uses.

At the end of each month, it is a good idea to compare receivables and payables. If payables are greater than receivables, that reflects negative cash flow. When receivables are greater than payables, positive cash flow is indicated. Accounts receivable should be 5 percent to 25 percent greater than accounts payable on a monthly comparable basis, depending on margins.

Be sure to audit all supplier invoices for accuracy in unit pricing, quantity (count), and specification. Check all deliveries for damage before signing the manifest or delivery receipt.

Chapter 4

ACCOUNTS RECEIVABLE

It is equally blessed to receive as it is to pay.

Accounts receivable is all about managing credit, having sensible invoicing and collection policies, and enforcing incoming cash flow at maximum levels. This means that someone in your company needs to be assigned to communicating with all customers, whether or not they are delinquent.

Accounts receivable are the lifeblood of the company in the form of cash flow. Cash flow of most companies is thought to be in good shape if it is between twenty-five and thirty-five days (DSO or day sales outstanding), depending on your company's credit terms. In many retail companies, DSO does not apply when sales are for cash or credit card.

Terms will vary regarding whether your company is retail, wholesale, manufacturing, or service-oriented. Margins, inventory turns, fixed and variable expenses, and other considerations also affect terms of sale.

Credit managers should maintain a sequence of contacts including letters (often called dun letters), phone calls, personal calls, and negotiations. The credit manager should be empowered to make "deals" with delinquent customers such as portions of past-due invoices that must be collected for each shipment delivery and other techniques for receiving payment. The imposition of late fees may be of assistance in collections, but these fees should be negotiable as long as the risk of receiving payment does not increase.

Some marginal customers will max out their credit limit with one supplier and then turn to another supplier for purchases. This type of customer bounces back and forth from supplier to supplier with little hope of catching up their payables. When this happens (or may be happening), the credit manager should feel free to check with other suppliers regarding their transactions with the customer in question. Be warned that calls or communications of this sort cannot be conspiratorial, for that is unlawful. It is legal to give and receive information about credit, sales, and other data, but agreements of how customers will be dealt with must not be made. Agreement between competing companies regarding price and terms of sale to customers are absolutely prohibited.

Chapter 5

ADVERTISING

Optimism must be tempered with reality.

Advertising is a universal need for businesses of all sizes. There are many ways advertising can benefit a business and their products or services. Remember that advertising is an expense. The only reason to spend money is to generate profit; thus, money spent on advertising should always pass the test of producing more profit than it costs. That simply means that for each dollar spent on advertising, you should expect a return of more than one dollar in profit. Generally, you should expect to get many times the advertising expense in net profit.

When you commit company financial resources to advertising agencies or direct to media, be sure to have a system in place that will tell you about your return on investment (ROI). There are many ways to evaluate the effectiveness of advertising spending by making sure you always ask prospects and customers how they heard about your company and/or its products and services. Insist on participation in evaluating the effectiveness by the agency or the media being used (newspaper, magazine, TV, radio, Internet, other).

Be very careful about the formal agreement or contract for advertising services. Let's say that you sign a one-year agreement for a specific level of advertising with your local TV station for $18,000. But let's say that only a single sale amounting to $350 can be traced to this advertising agreement during the first six months. You believe your advertising dollars are being wasted, and you want to exit the agreement before the year is over. Make sure you deal with this possibility before signing the agreement. Always provide for an early exit when the evidence is clear that your advertising dollars are being squandered. You may want to have your attorney review the agreement and make suggestions for changing some wording and clauses.

Whether you deal directly with a media company or with an agency, make sure you receive demographic information prior to making any agreement. This simply means finding out who listens, watches, or reads the medium that is under consideration—the target audience that is most likely to be interested in considering and purchasing your specific products and/or services.

Perhaps the most valuable form of advertising is WOM or word of mouth. WOM advertising is most often created by satisfied customers who like your company's products and services. In some cases, WOM is created by people who have simply heard of your company's reputation. It behooves all entrepreneurs to do everything possible to foster as much WOM advertising as possible. It is highly effective and very low cost.

Other forms of advertising are newspapers, magazines, radio, television, Internet, direct mail, insertion in local shopping flyers, yard signs, telephone solicitation, door-to-door, signage in public places, and billboards. Advertising expenses often are about 5 percent of sales revenue.

Develop a reasonable advertising budget, but make sure the spending is flexible in the same manner as the impact and effectiveness of the advertising.

Chapter 6

ANTICIPATION

Don't cross bridges before you come to them, and don't burn them after crossing.

—Words from my mother

One of the greatest attributes a person can possess and employ is the ability to anticipate what others want or need. For example, a CFO or controller can add a lot of credibility to the job if he anticipates a report that the boss would like to see or an explanation about a financial anomaly that the bank needs to hear about.

The boss that anticipates the wants or needs of employees, suppliers, and customers can usually reap great rewards by researching the desires of important stakeholders and by acting on the evidence developed. A secretary or clerical worker can often receive favorable benefits by reporting information to the boss that had not surfaced before.

Be sure to read (sometimes between the lines) all economic, cultural, and industry signals that might have an impact on your business and its products and services. Anticipate necessary adjustments in company strategy.

Chapter 7

APPLICATION FOR JOBS

When accepting applications for job openings, make sure your questions always comply with all regulations and employment laws.

Some key points to remember are:

Use extreme caution when an applicant says that the reason for leaving one or more jobs in the past was: "My boss and I didn't get along" or "Disagreements with others in the company."
Be sure to question gaps in past employment of more than a few weeks. You should know why the person was out of work or what they were doing during a long period of unemployment.

Never allow an applicant to leave the building with an application. It must be filled out in the presence of a company employee.

Even if it is simple and brief, have a personnel manual that covers hours of work, layoff and separation (firing) policy, work expectations, sexual harassment, bullying, quality, productivity, safety and attitude, and other employment relationship details. An employer representative should read the personnel manual to newly hired employees and have them sign and date the document.

Make sure the hours of work are explained clearly and the penalties for being late or absent. Discuss all violations by employees and discuss the range of consequences.

Be sure to have photo ID on file for each employee. Verify citizenship or authorization to work in the USA.

See Appendix H for sample application.
See Chapter 31, Employee Manual.

Chapter 8

ATTITUDE

High morale contributes to a dynamic workplace.

Attitude, along with quality, productivity, and safety, comprise the core requirements for the continuous improvement and progress of every company. All these basic attributes must be practiced at all times, every day by everyone in the company—no exceptions.

Attitude is not something that can be demanded, required, or insisted upon. It is a condition that is native to every individual. Attitude is the collective mind-set of persons who are at peace with themselves, their families and friends, and their job.

Attitude can be adjusted and swayed internally by individuals when a company culture is one of mutual respect, reasoned discipline, and results orientation.

Good attitudes are usually created in a work environment where loud talk, screaming, and profanity are not acceptable and not used.

A company's culture becomes ingrained over time when attitudes are positive because all levels of authority and work are melded into daily routines of positive input and output.

Chapter 9

ATTORNEYS (LAWYERS)

Free advice: Good lawyers make and keep timetables; don't accept vague or evasive dates of fulfillment of obligations and agreements.

At some point in the creation and operation of your business, there will be a need for an attorney. Ask some questions throughout the business community, especially others whose businesses are about your size in annual sales, number of employees, and overall profile. When you have developed information about possible legal advisors, request an interview with several of them. Make sure you feel "comfortable" with the legal advisor that will cost you real money but will also save you from legal pitfalls that face all business people

It is important that you know and understand the fees that will be charged for various services. If the attorney does not have a list of fees, make sure you write them down and file them for future reference. Find out the hourly cost of legal advice as well as the cost for research and the hourly rate charged for secretaries and paralegals. Be sure to know cost of representation at trial in case a courtroom visit should occur.

Ask the attorney about the range of services he/she or "the firm" can handle. For example, the law as related to wages and hours, union organizing, personal injury, credit/collections, and document reviews (employee handbooks, lease agreements, real estate transactions, wills, medical directives, estate planning, general business transactions).

It is also worthwhile to make clear the value of your time. When you have an appointment with your attorney, you should expect the meeting to start promptly. If you are left to wait more than a few minutes, you should explain your objection and suggest that in the future, your wait time should not exceed your expectations.

Here's a partial list of fee information you should inquire about:

1. The cost per hour of a conference with an attorney.
2. The cost per hour for secretarial transcribing, letter-writing, and other clerical duties.
3. The cost of collections, courtroom appearances, and associated work regarding collections.
4. The cost of collections based on hours or percentage when contingency fees are involved.
5. Cost of telephone calls by the minute or fractional hour.

Insist on receiving on-time performance relating to all legal matters.

Chapter 10

BANKING

Honesty is the best policy. (Cultural comment heard round the world)

There is an old, tired saying about banks that goes like this: "Banks will loan you money when you don't need it but will withhold funds when you do need them."

That is often true but only when the borrower probably hasn't kept the bank informed of the financial and operating status of the company. For example, a business that has developed losses over the past several months without alerting their bank may have more trouble borrowing money to meet payroll this Friday because the bank was not aware of the cash flow situation. In every case when a business owner needs an emergency injection of cash, the bank will need to assess the risks of increasing their capital investment in your company.

When you open the doors of your new business or are considering changing banks, bring along the latest balance sheet, profit and loss statement, and possibly a cash flow analysis. Tell them about mistakes of the past and opportunities for the future. Be candid.

For best relations with your bank, provide a balance sheet and a profit and loss statement monthly. No matter how good or bad the month was, provide this and other critical information. When you have suffered a loss or other negative condition, tell the bank, outline the problem, and then explain how the problem is being resolved with the least injury to the company.

Wining and dining is not essential, but honesty and straightforward information is necessary. Your banking relationship will flourish when they are treated as a partner rather than as an adversary.

See Chapter 84, SWOT; and Chapter 37, Financial Statements.

Chapter 11

Best Practices (Benchmarks)

Quality must be under constant repair and maintenance

Best practices, also known as benchmarks, are the records over time that are kept of various company functions. Here are a few benchmarks that could (should) be kept:

- Weekly, monthly, annual sales
- Cost of mistakes and errors in administration, maintenance, production, sales
- Productivity overall and direct
- Miles driven compared with gross revenue and sales, installations, and other off-site functions.

By keeping records of various functions, it can be easily determined what teams are the most efficient, what people are the most productive, and what processes could be eliminated or changed.

Keep benchmark data and discuss it regularly with staff. Make appropriate changes.

Chapter 12

BREAKEVEN

Fact: Profit is generated only when gross profit percent is greater than expense percent.

This is a very important number. Your company makes no profit during any period of time, such as a month, until breakeven sales revenue is reached. The breakeven point changes from month to month because of changes in gross profit and expenses. Cost of goods sold or COGS usually represents variable costs while expenses are fixed, variable, and mixed costs.

Computing your company breakeven should be done each month as soon as the financial reports are prepared. While there are several ways of computing breakeven for specific months, the most simple and accurate method is as follows:

To compute breakeven for any period, simply divide the gross profit (GP) by total sales revenue. The result is a decimal amount less than one (1). Divide the decimal amount into the amount of total expenses. The result is the breakeven for the selected period. Examples:

Total Revenue for January:	$370,000
Cost of Goods Sold (COGS):	$255,000
Gross Profit:	$115,000
Total Expenses:	$121,000

Divide GP of $115,000 by $370,000 = .3108 = 31.08%

Divide Expenses of $121,000 by .3108 = $389,318 = Breakeven (BE)

This calculation shows that BE was greater by more than $19,000 than revenue for the month of January and reflects the company loss for the month.

Another example:

Total Revenue for April: $435,000

Cost of Goods Sold (COGS): $265,000

Gross Profit (GP): $170,000

Total Expenses: $146,000

Divide GP of $170,000 by $435,000 = .3908 = 39.08%

Divide Total Expense of $146,000 by .3908 = $373,593 = Breakeven (BE)

This calculation shows that the BE was less than actual revenue generated for April, and thus the company generated a profit. Note that the company was losing money on every sale during the month until the GP was exactly equal to the expenses that had occurred during the month.

In every breakeven month, the company is actually losing from 2 percent to 5 percent because of the time value of money (invested funds). In other words, precise breakeven volume represents a slight loss for the period considering the time/value of money.

Chapter 13

BUREAUCRACY

Successful entrepreneurs often have a rich mix of scientific objectivity and artistic engagement.

As your company grows and generates increased profits, there is a predilection to slip into the complexity of bureaucratic management. Bureaucracies are staffed by bureaucrats, and bureaucrats often generate more heat than light. That is, many bureaucrats become paper shufflers, rumor-mongers, time wasters, and "redundancy experts." Here are some symptoms to watch for:

- A new vehicle is ordered because it looks nice, and we may need it someday.
- Additional electronic equipment is installed because two people agreed that the equipment would make great management tools.
- To complement the computers, printers, and other new electronic equipment, additional specialized software is installed without knowing exactly how it will benefit the company.
- More data is developed and distributed than can be effectively used by those who want it, need it, or think they want it or need it.
- New people with special skills for operating new machines and equipment are hired with earnings at new, higher levels. The new hires have nebulous achievement goals that are not measurable.
- The administration budget is increased multiple times during a short period, such as a few months or a year. Example: An employee's son or daughter is hired to get and sort the mail. The job requires two hours, but the pay is for eight hours.

- Expenses increase, margins decrease, profits decline. Management says sales are going to increase; we are not sure how or when or why, but we are fairly sure sales are going to increase.

Some defenses against becoming too bureaucratic are as follows:

- Every capital investment in new equipment is offset by increased efficiency and resulting profits within twenty-four months using reasonable, conservative assumptions.
- The cost of every new employee is compensated by improved productivity and resulting profits within ninety days. The efforts of every employee must result in more profitability than the total compensation and benefits awarded to that employee.
- If the timing and the profit contributions do *not* work out as mentioned above, you have paid too much for the person(s) or the equipment, or the functions were unnecessary in part or in whole.

Apply zero-based budgeting at the beginning of every calendar or fiscal year. Zero-based budgeting requires the amounts in each line item to be justified and validated and often removes unnecessary redundant spending.

Taken to extremes, bureaucracy transforms dreams into nightmares by slowing the process of decision making, by using false assumptions, by unleashing biased opinions, and by adding surplus people, processes, and investments without a reasonable return on investment.

Make sure your business bureaucracy eliminates bias and achieves maximum results.

Chapter 14

BUSINESS PLAN

A business plan is similar to planning all the ingredients for the recipe that promises a cake.

Every enterprise should create an annual business plan. Although any plan amounts to an educated guess, a plan provides guidance in sales, budgeting, and all other aspects of the business.

Business plans start with the sales forecast. Consider all aspects of sales and marketing with forecasts by sales people, customer service representatives, and others that have a "feel" for sales and marketing.

Next, make a complete list of cost of materials plus freight in and labor; this is cost of goods sold or COGS. This category of labor is all labor costs associated directly with production or services for billing.

Now make a list of all fixed expenses such as rent, insurance, utilities, maintenance, and other expenses.

Add the cost of administrative labor and salaries not involved with direct production including payroll expenses and taxes.

Add all other items of expense such as fuel costs, waste disposal, legal, accountancy, fees, commissions, bonuses, licenses, entertainment, and supplies (office and other).

As each month passes, compare actual sales and expenses with budget and make adjustments.

Each year should have a new zero-based budget to follow throughout the year. Avoid using last year's budget with estimated additions and deductions. Doing that tends to favor spending and often overlooks thrift.

Chapter 15

BUY OR LEASE

Buying is investing; leasing is expensing.

When procuring nonresale items subject to depreciation such as vehicles, machines, and other operating equipment, there are generally four methods of acquisition:

- Purchase for cash.
- Purchase "on time" by making a down payment and the balance of the cost over one to several years.
- True lease means that you or your company does not accept ownership of the item but rather the utilization of the item is exchanged for regular payments over a period of time. At the end of the lease period, the vehicle or other equipment can be returned to the lease-holder. In many cases, the lessee can purchase the item at an agreed-upon market price.
- Capitalized lease. When this deal is transacted, the monthly payments are established along with a "buyout" price at the termination of the "lease". The "lessee" takes ownership of the item and agrees there is an accompanying obligation to purchase the item at the previously agreed-upon residual price at the end of the payment period. This leasing method is similar to buying "on time" or using a promissory note.

Be sure to discuss the various methods of purchase with your accountant to make sure all tax liabilities are accommodated and the lowest overall cost is received. When acquiring equipment or real estate, make sure you understand all aspects of the transactions.

Each of these acquisition methods has its advantages. Purchasing equipment for cash is usually the lowest cost route to ownership. It is often easier to negotiate a lower overall cost price with the seller. Also, if the buyer uses available cash, interest costs are avoided, making substantial savings.

When purchasing equipment or vehicles using a promissory note, it may be more difficult to obtain a lower purchase price; and when interest payments are added to the cost of the item, the true cost of the addition is considerably more than the "sticker" price.

As a rule of thumb, vehicles or equipment purchased should return cost savings sufficient to liquidate the price of the investment in twenty-four months. If that formula doesn't work out for new purchases, consider used vehicles or equipment.

Vehicles, especially large trucks and heavy equipment, are expensive. If margins are relatively high, you can consider having a "true" lease. If your margins are low and sensitive, you may want to consider purchasing vehicles with notes that extend over thirty-six months or longer. Another option is the capitalized "lease" mentioned above.

It is always useful to discuss and compare the various methods of equipment acquisition with the seller or dealer.

Chapter 16

CAPITAL INVESTMENT

All debt must be eventually liquidated unless bankruptcy intervenes.

Especially during the early years of operation, monitor debt obligations carefully. Initial capital investment at the time of startup usually includes inventory, equipment, displays, and perhaps expense of lease improvements. Here are some suggestions:

Set up with bank or other lending partner funding covering fixed expenses such as leasehold improvements, equipment, and other items that have a year or more of durability and use.

Regarding inventory, it is often favorable to establish a line of credit that will cover the ups and downs of inventory investment. Using a line of credit, you can pay interest on the varying amounts of borrowed capital to maintain optimum inventory investment and control.

Now let's say that you will need a panel delivery vehicle for pickup and delivery items. Suppose you settle on a new fourteen-foot box van that is available from a local dealer for $38,000 at 3.9 percent interest for four years. The monthly payment will amount to $856.30 plus the cost of insurance. Go to a local dealer or get on line and suppose we find a three-year-old model similar to the new one with forty thousand miles on it in good shape. The dealer is asking $18,000 for this vehicle. At this price, with interest a little higher at 4.2 percent, for two years, the payments will be $783.25 plus insurance for twenty-four months.

Which is the better buy? Consider that note payments will be lower on the used vehicle; insurance may be slightly lower, maintenance will probably be a little higher, but you will have the title to the vehicle in half the time had you purchased the new vehicle. The cash outlay for the new vehicle would be $41,102 and for the used van, the outlay would amount to $18,798.

A good rule of thumb for the addition of vehicles, machinery, and other operating equipment should return the cost of investment in savings and productivity in two years or less, especially with young companies. To arrive at the earning power of an asset, consider the savings in labor and time (increased efficiency and output), customer benefits and reduced waste, and other efficiencies and assign reasonable values to these benefits. Match the benefit to the cost of the capital investment and pay it off in twenty-four months or less.

Heavy fixed machines often have a useful life of ten years or more. Most trucks and commercial vehicles have a useful life of four to six years; automobiles will operate reasonably well for one hundred twenty thousand miles or more when properly serviced and maintained. Because of the rapidly changing upgrades and changes in computers, printers, copiers, and other office equipment, the useful life can range from a couple years to (at most) about five years.

The important criterion to remember about capital investment is *never* owe money for a machine or vehicle that is at the end of its useful productive life.

Chapter 17

CELEBRATIONS!

Those who overestimate themselves often underestimate others.

Everybody loves a party to celebrate something. Birthdays make great celebration themes. It might be a good idea to have a birthday cake monthly for all birthdays during that month. Other celebrations can be when a product is kicked off or introduced. Have a party when the new wing of the shop or office is completed. Celebrate perfect attendance or no tardiness for a year. Offer gift certificates or simply congratulatory certificates to give to employees along with recognition in their personnel files. Celebrate a special achievement or accomplishment by an employee. This can be some kind of community or social recognition or something related to company activities.

Celebrate winning if your company fields a softball team, a bowling team, or other athletic activity. The company has probably subsidized shirts, uniforms, or caps for participants. If an employee is a member of the local band or chorus, recognize their participation in the activity.

Never forget that without high-quality employees, there is no company. Expensive machines and computers, loads of inventory, and a customer list amounting to countless numbers have no value without productive employees.

Workers at all levels love to see their names and photos in the local paper or the company newsletter.
Think morale!

Chapter 18

CHANGE

People deplore change because of uncertainty; they adjust with satisfaction when results are favorable.

Always do your best to get out in front of "change." Products, technology, taxes, the economy, buying trends, and other changes are going on at all times. Business leaders must be constantly evaluating product changes and trends, laws, population shifts, and other factors that affect every business.

Automobile factories have closed because their leaders failed to change their offerings to meet the demands of customer needs. Airline companies have folded in the face of competition and changing habits of travelers. Companies that stood firm against emerging technologies have failed.

On the other hand, there are companies that got too far "out front" and got into financial and operating trouble by being "ahead of the curve" of the pesky immutable laws of supply and demand.

Change is as certain as day and night. All companies must adjust to it in a timely manner. Be a benefactor of change, not a victim of it.

Chapter 19

CHARITABLE DONATIONS

Some economists feel that corporate leaders have a responsibility to make charitable contributions on their own and preserve corporate capital for investors and employees.

It is true that capital profits become the domain of company leaders, owners (stockholders), and employees (compensation). It is therefore the jurisdiction of company leaders to spend those profits where the company's value will be most greatly enhanced.

At the local level, that may be baseball caps, T-shirts, and a host of other donations to charitable organizations. However, if a company president or CEO wants to donate a million bucks to his alma mater, that should be his or her own funds derived from compensation or investment income.

One of the most valuable ways to participate in local fund drives is by asking for voluntary donations by employees along with larger sums by company leaders.

It is unwise and even unethical to make political donations through the company because company leaders are fiduciaries of employees, and investors making such contributions (by proxy) are possible disagreement with the political people or policies being contributed to.

Chapter 20

COMMUNICATIONS

Proverb: Ask questions when you don't know the answers but sometimes when you do.

When someone tells you that they will call you about some issue on Tuesday, you should reasonably expect them to call next Tuesday, right? In real life, how often does that actually happen? When you go to a customer's place of business for a 3:00 p.m. meeting on Wednesday, November 3 and the customer forgot about the meeting appointment, you have wasted some valuable time. If you show up for a doctor's appointment on Tuesday at 10:00 a.m. and the receptionist or nurse tells you the appointment was for tomorrow, there was a misunderstanding. Time was wasted.

When a communication commitment is made, be sure to keep that commitment. Tell those with whom you work that your expectations for them are the same. Lack of quality communications is one of the important reasons that some people and businesses fall into the category of mediocrity.

Tips:

- If someone tells you they will call Monday but don't call, call them on Tuesday.

- Return all missed calls as soon as possible. Always call within twenty-four hours, no matter how busy you are.

- When you make an appointment for a "few minutes," make sure you keep looking at your watch and terminate the meeting in a "few minutes." This usually means less than ten minutes.

- Incoming phone calls are always made at a time convenient for the caller. If you are busy, decline the call and return the call when convenient for yourself.

- Do not make commitments that you can't or won't keep.

- Be precise and punctual about all communications and expect the same courtesy of others.

Chapter 21

COMPENSATION: HOURLY

A worker must always produce more value than earned compensation and benefits.

Hourly workers are truly the backbone of every company participating in the nation's industrial/commercial output. Hourly employees are the essence of unpretentious humility. Hourly workers are smart in their own way, so bosses, supervisors, and managers should never lie to them or take them for granted.

When workers understand their jobs, the company goals, and reasonable expectations, most individuals will work very productively. Training from day one is always effective in helping an average worker to become an exceptional one.

When any worker does not improve in all areas of work assignments, provide additional remedial training. If that doesn't improve the worker's work habits and quality output, it's time to suggest a career change. Releasing hard-working but inept workers is hard, but the company and other employees will be better off.

Every hourly worker must have measurable results to achieve. Whether in sales, production, maintenance, any job in the company must have measurable results.

Upon hiring, make an offer of wages at the low end of the scale with promises of increases upon learning and performing job assignments. The first review and evaluation should be in thirty days and the next one in sixty or ninety days. If there is no improvement in thirty days, the employee should become a former employee with a pat on the back and a few words of well-wishes.

The sixty- or ninety-day review and evaluation should include increased compensation or promotion or both. This is important: never fail to review an employee on schedule; this reflects respect for the worker and his skilled efforts. This is called "building rapport."

Chapter 22

COMPENSATION: SALARIED

If you seek loyalty, get a dog.

Because the rules for compensation and benefits change so frequently at all levels of government, no specific details will be offered in this chapter. Be sure to check with your local State Employment Commission for details and follow the rules meticulously. It's too expensive and time consuming to run afoul of employment legislation at the federal or state level.

Some common sense rules should be heeded. When you hire a salaried employee, make sure a measurable set of expectations are agreed upon. Usually, a salaried person will be hired at the lower range of salaries with promises of increases as skill levels and quality output increases.

It is usually wise to set a couple chronological points of review and evaluation, one within thirty days and the other about sixty or ninety days away. In the event that the employee shows no measurable progress within thirty days, it is time to help the employee find alternative employment.

At the sixty- or ninety-day review and evaluation, be sure to dig deep into details and make sure that the worker finds the job to be challenging, that working with coworkers is pleasant.

The first raise or promotion (or both) may be appropriate at this time. Make sure that compensation for all employees produce value greater than their compensation and benefits. Be sure that each employee is aware of the need to save part of their compensation for investing in the future, specifically retirement income and benefits.

The time value of employees, both salaried and hourly, should be evaluated and compensated according to their contributions to the company bottom line. The employee that has been with the company for twenty years should be paid no more than the worker with equal or superior skills that has been with the company a shorter period of time. The long-term employee should enjoy benefits of company seniority but based only on productivity, not tenure.

Chapter 23

COMPETITION

Competition is a great teacher.

Competition comes in many forms: price, service, quality, location, courtesy, and in combinations of all factors of difference (differentiation).

Every business should have an accurate handle on the competitiveness of their product or service offerings. In our capitalist style of commerce, competition is the spice of differentiation. What applies to automobiles and X-ray machines also applies to nearly every product or service. It is imperative for each business person to be on constant alert to make their products and services more attractive to shoppers that can be converted to buyers, especially repeat buyers.

For example, the car you have for sale may be about the same price as the car being offered by another dealer a mile or so away. Each of these dealers must strive to find what features, both major and minor, will make a difference in the purchasing decision of prospective buyers.

With impulse items such as boxes of sugar, a commodity, the difference in a customer's perception may be in the packaging. The decision for a bicyclist to purchase one bike over another may be in the warranty. For the buyer of a huge class "8" diesel truck or power unit, part of the decision may rest on the lighter weight of one unit, allowing it to carry more cargo. Vacationers might purchase one canoe or kayak over another because of the perception of safety over price. A casual buyer of a loaf of bread may be motivated to pay a dollar more for a loaf at a convenience store rather than drive another couple of miles to the supermarket.

Perhaps the most important consideration regarding competition is the perceived value of one product over other similar offerings. Products that have a highly favorable reputation often are a little more profitable for the seller than lesser known products.

Remember the rule of reputation: it usually take years to build a strong reputation but only a short time to shred that reputation through a careless mistake or incorrect assumption. It is called the "snowball effect." It is a tedious job to make a huge snowball by rolling damp snow uphill, but one push and that ball rolls back downhill at increasing speed and often disintegrates at the bottom of the hill.

Chapter 24

COMPUTERS

Moore's Law: The processing power of computers will double about every two years.

This chapter is almost superfluous because nearly every business has one or more computers with appropriate software.

Here are some general tips regarding computers:

1. Back up everything of importance. There are companies that specialize in automatically backing up all or portions of your work. And of course, there are many ways that a company can establish internal backup, either manual or automatic. Don't suffer a loss by forgetting to backup critical data!

2. There are voluminous reports of computer abuse by employees. There may be romantic messages to other employees, playing of games, surfing the web, viewing pornography or illegal sites such as child porn, bomb and weapons making, etc. If you suspect anyone of wasting time or using the computer for malicious activity, it is best to alert authorities and engage a specialist that works with computer data controls and forensics. Establish firm policies regarding personal computer use by employees.

3. Don't wait for a system failure to establish a relationship with a computer repair and maintenance specialist. Have available the names of at least two people or companies that can be secured on short notice.

4. Because technology changes so rapidly, make sure your software and hardware are updated periodically. Time and quality can be wasted by hanging onto old hardware and software beyond their most efficient operating term.

5. If you think you can get along without a computer, try one out for several months, and you will find that a computer is indispensable in businesses of every size and type.

Chapter 25

CONSULTANTS

Those who believe they never need help are deceiving themselves.

When you need help running your company, you may want to call in a consultant or a consulting firm. There are those who present themselves as consultants and have little experience or knowledge to help solve your problems. Consulting firms and individual advisors are usually expensive. If you decide to engage a consultant, make sure you know exactly what is going to happen. Here are some guidelines:

- Put in writing exactly what kind of help you want. State what you want the result of their assistance and advice to be.
- Require consultants and/or consulting firms to put in written form their understanding of the goals you have outlined.
- Insist on the time in days, weeks, or months that the project is expected to take. Do not leave open-ended start and finish dates and times.
- Make a list of the consulting firm's hourly fees, out-of-pocket expenses, and all other fees and when payments are expected (up-front, daily, weekly, monthly, points of progress, etc.).
- Some consultants are prone to offer their services using key words and phrases that may be industry jargon and/or double talk. Make sure there is clear understanding in all aspects of the agreement and the association. Think in terms of straightforward simplicity of communication and activity.
- Insist on an escape clause. If little progress is noted within agreed-upon time boundaries, stop wasting your money and sever the agreement.
- It is often appropriate to direct contracts to your attorney with instructions about escape clauses and other safety features.

Chapter 26

COSTS AND EXPENSES

Gross Profit (GP) is the difference between cost of goods sold (COGS) and sell; net profit or net loss is the difference between GP and expenses.

For the purposes in this handbook, costs and expenses are distinguished by their origination and attachment. The following is the meaning of these two similar words:

Costs: These are the product costs that are included in cost of goods sold. The product or service cost can include freight in at your discretion. Costs include all direct labor, but for the purposes of this manual, costs do *not* include indirect costs such as administration (bookkeeping, building maintenance, etc.).

Expenses: These are the items that include spending that is usually not traceable to a particular product or function. Expenses can include "fixed" such as insurance, maintenance, trash disposal, energy for heating, lighting and air conditioning, and rent.

There is usually a "variable" component to fixed expenses such as energy costs, insurance, and fuel for vehicles based on the number of miles traveled, the hours the building is heated or air conditioned and lighted.

Some expenses are a mix of fixed and variable. For example, workman's compensation insurance is required but varies with changes in payroll. Cost of waste disposal is a requirement for most businesses but varies with the amount of waste generated daily, weekly, and monthly. Fuel and vehicle and equipment maintenance varies with miles driven and operating hours for equipment.

Ask your accountant for further explanations unique to your set of financial records.

Chapter 27

CREDIT MANAGEMENT

Old saying: In God we trust; all others cash.

Credit management has huge penalties and just as huge rewards. Ineffective cash management retards cash flow and strains the financial integrity of the company. One of the strains it imposes is cash for paying suppliers on time and the taking of cash (prompt payment) discounts.

Whether credit management is a full-time or part-time job, there has to be a fairly strict system in place to maintain prompt timely cash resources to gnaw away at short-term liabilities and long-term debt. These obligations require timely liquidation that usually requires payment of interest on debt. Some suppliers, for example, have delinquency fees amounting to 1.5 percent or 2 percent per month. When annualized, these rates work out to be 18 percent and 24 percent annually. That makes for expensive delinquency.

Many retail operations require cash, checks, or credit card purchases that enhance cash flow. The caution here is to avoid losses of bad checks and bogus or stolen credit cards. Cameras, photo IDs, and other requirements can usually hold down losses from these forms of payments that are made at the time of sale. Obviously, cash (no credit) businesses have flexibility of pricing and margins because of cash float—some items get sold before reimbursing supplier—delinquency risk (slow pay), and deadbeat customers.

Credit management in wholesale and manufacturing sales is more complicated. Usually companies offer terms of thirty days with 1 percent or 2 percent cash discount if paid within thirty days. These suppliers often have late payment fees of 1.5 percent to 2 percent per month on delinquent payments. When customers don't pay on time, the first notice of late payment is often a card or letter of request for payment. The second follow-up is sometimes a phone call. Depending on geographic location, the next contact should be either personal or by phone of a company official. As a last resort, it may be necessary to get an attorney involved. Most attorneys will show you how to file claims and pursue collections without paying for costly legal intervention. Use extreme caution if you decide to engage a collection agency.

A cautionary note about litigation to collect funds: lawyers, court costs, and your time are costly. If, for example, a customer owes your company $3,000 and the cost of litigation is $5,000, you may win the case but lose $2,000. Plan ahead and be cautious regarding the cost of litigation related to delinquent funds to be collected.

There are many techniques for collecting slow-paying customers. One solution is to place their account on COD plus a portion of the past due balance. Another plan is to insist on regular payments using a registered promissory note. For companies that sell into the construction industry, a property lien can usually be placed against projects under construction.

In Internet sales, vendors often use a Web-related service like PayPal to assure receipt of timely payment. The important consideration about credit management is this: in order to pay suppliers within thirty days, you must collect from your customers in no more than twenty-five days. For those customers who scream that you've got to give them ninety days to pay, your company may be better off without their business. Life is short (and so is cash)!

Chapter 28

DIVERSIONS

Self-improvement can be achieved by helping others.

There are many ways to spend money at the behest of others. Sales people have offers that you can't refuse. Really? The product or service being offered will produce unbelievable profits and benefits for your company. Really?

When unbelievable offers are made, they often are (unbelievable). Ask some questions. Here are some samples:

1. Are special introductory terms offered?
2. If sales don't materialize, can inventory be returned at full cost?
3. Is the product warranted?
4. Is the supplier responsible with a good reputation?
5. What promotional materials are supplied?
6. What is the history and record of other recent companies selling these products or services?

The point is that if a new project or service is being considered, make sure it fits into the business plan and product strategy of your company. There are thousands, perhaps millions of companies that have been unsuccessful with new products and services and have lost sums of money that could have been spent more wisely.

On the other hand, new products and services can bring vitality to company offerings and should be given the test of "fit" with company business plan and additional profit. Always consider the needs of your company over the needs of the person and company making the offer.

Diversions into new opportunities are good only when they contribute to your bottom line.

Other forms of diversion include pointless lunches, dinners, and breakfasts. Why waste two hours or more talking about politics, the new police chief, or ice melt in Polar Regions? If someone wants to sell you a product or service you are not interested in, don't waste an hour telling the person that you are not interested. You can courteously explain your disinterest in two or three minutes and allow the visitor to go elsewhere and waste someone else's time.

Chapter 29

DIVERSITY

Hire associates on the basis of potential or proven skills; diversity will follow.

Diversity by race, gender, sexual orientation, and handicap status is a wonderful, often fulfilling goal for any company, large or small. However, don't be hoodwinked into believing that diversity is good just for the sake of diversity. The fundamental motive for all firms that are not organized for purely charitable purposes should be to make a profit. Profit rewards proprietors, partners, or shareholders for the risk they have incurred by investing in assets to produce products and services to generate a profit.

Diversity in any organization can be achieved very comprehensively by hiring people using one of two criteria. First, a person can be hired because they possess the knowledge and skills to help maintain or improve the level of performance of the enterprise. The other reason for hiring a person is that the prospective employee has the potential for learning the necessary skills to enhance the company's growth and profitability.

To insure diversity, interview a broad range of candidates. Don't allow stereotyping into the interviewing and hiring process. For example, women are now police officers and EMS professionals, truck drivers, and corporate CEOs. Men are entering occupations such as Registered Nurses and LPNs, hairdressers, and "house husbands." Blacks, Orientals, and Hispanics can be found in positions of great responsibility throughout our country and the world. Giant steps have been made in helping women and men do amazing feats in spite of amputations and other "handicaps."

Age, gender, race, religion, handicap status, sexual orientation, or ethnicity should not ever be considered a bar to employing any person. The question of prior criminal records has been stricken from all federal job application forms, and some smaller jurisdictions have followed suit. While appearance is a strong indicator of a person's acuity, ignore race, gender, accent, and other characteristics that could disqualify an otherwise highly qualified person.

Discrimination in hiring and in employment by any company is against the law.

Chapter 30

DRUGS (ILLICIT)

Users of illicit drugs should be prohibited from using drugs on company time, on company premises, or in company vehicles. Violators should be warned on hiring day and fired on using day.

Any conversation in any business about drugs should be simple and straightforward. Drugs are *not* allowed in the workplace or on the premises. We have all read or seen the havoc that drugs can inflict on a person, a family, a company, a community, or an organization of any kind.

Check with your local police, sheriff's office, or other law enforcement organization in your area and find out and employ the rules for drug testing. The rules of personal privacy and company safety and responsibility must be considered and respected.

It might be appropriate to do random drug testing of one or more individuals on a rotating basis. In most cases, it is probably more fitting to test individuals without notice that are exhibiting erratic behavior or showing signs of sudden personality changes. Be sure random testing is truly random to avoid the possibility of gender or racial bias.

In summary, illicit drugs simply should not be used at any time by any employees for any reason. If anyone in the organization suspects drug use by anyone, that person should report the evidence immediately. It is logical that anyone using alcoholic beverages or illicit drugs is more prone to accident and injury whether operating a machine, driving a vehicle, riding a desk, or operating a broom or floor buffer. Accidents are costly beyond your wildest nightmares. See Chapter 1, Accidents; and Chapter 78, Safety.

Owners and managers should set the example of *not using illicit drugs*. Remember that some people are at risk of developing dependency on prescription drugs. If you or anyone in your organization continues using a prescription medication for a long period of time, abuse can result.

The key is *zero tolerance for illicit drugs.*

Chapter 31

EMPLOYEE MANUAL

Exercise the discipline of boundaries.

If you have but one employee, an employee manual should be created and kept available for review and change as necessary.

An employee manual should contain information about the relationship between employer and employee. Here are some issues that should be covered:

Compensation policy
Hours of operation
Attire (dress code) expectations
Conditions of employment (at will, contract, etc.)
Smoking, nonsmoking on premises
Prohibition of illicit drug use on and off premises
Prohibition of alcohol use on premises
Vacation allowances
Sick leave allowances
Access to buildings and limitations (keys, alarm codes)
Violations and consequences (smoking, drinking, etc.)
Rules of harassment (sexual, gender, bullying)

Ideas for simple employee handbooks are available from other companies in your area, on the Internet, and from the library. If you belong to a trade association, their office may have helpful information. As each employee is introduced to the

"Employee Handbook," it should be signed by the employee and a representative of the employer to confirm knowledge and understanding.

It is not possible to define in writing the elements for the perfect company culture. A positive company culture is developed and perpetuated by an aura of success, satisfaction, completion, respect, discipline, and honesty.

Chapter 32

ENTREPRENEURSHIP

An independent business is never wholly independent; dependence on others is crucial to success.

Many men and women who form their own business have come from highly structured bureaucracies such as big business or government. Some give the reason that they are sick and tired of being bossed around and thus want to be their "own boss."

Sounds great, doesn't it? There are some important considerations to remember. First, when you were in a structured, bureaucratic job, there was a set of rules and a long list of policies that employees adhered to. Vacations, sick leave policy, retirement, and other details of the employer/employee relationship were specific and detailed.

Suddenly now, you must make your own rules and regulations. As boss, you must establish policies regarding all aspects of the employment relationship. Whatever policies and rules you create must be legal, ethical, and even-handed. See Chapter 31, Employee Manual.

An advantage to being an entrepreneur is that you can prioritize your own time, spend your money where you want to, and take vacations when it pleases your fancy.

This is where entrepreneurs must be cautious. You should think twice if Al calls and asks you to play golf if you must cancel an important meeting to accede to his request. You must avoid canceling an important employee meeting to go shopping with a friend. If you belong to a service club (Kiwanis, Lions, Rotary, etc.), you may have to skip a meeting occasionally when a key business decision must be made or an important meeting is scheduled

Especially during the startup stage of business formation and development, entrepreneurs must keep both feet on the ground, their nose to the grindstone, and their mind focused on profitable total performance.

Chapter 33

ETHICS

The practice of ethics is usually doing the right thing at the right time in the right place.

For most business owners and managers, ethical conduct is a given with no compromise. There may come the time in any person's business or personal life when the temptation to make some form of compromise of ethical principles is tested. Don't succumb to your inner desires!

Truth telling, honest dealing, and respect for opposing viewpoints is the rule of the day.

Over the long run, ethical demeanor pays huge dividends.

Chapter 34

EXIT STRATEGY I (HIRING A MANAGER)

Fact: All businesses change hands.

When you want to lessen the load of running the company on a day-to-day basis, you should appoint a trusted person with a strategic vision that is parallel with yours. If you are simply cutting down on the time you want to spend with customers, employees, and suppliers, determine exactly what the extent of effort you want to expend. Do you want to spend one day a week concentrating on the business and the rest of the time in the garden, on the golf course, or fishing?

Candidates that are the most likely leaders are present employees that have shown promise as strong managers/leaders.

Whatever your retirement or semiretirement plans, identify how much time you can allocate for your business. Then decide what functions you can provide with all other business activities controlled by another person—the manager.

Here is the most valuable advice you can heed: make sure your manager is results- or outcome-oriented. It is fundamental to realize that some very good managers perform tasks and chart courses and strategies differently than others. Keep your nose out of small details in favor of asking questions about overall plans, execution, and follow-up.

Set up reporting rules and adhere to them strictly. There are numerous incidents that relate to embezzlement or the faulty and downright dishonest activities that can be carried on by a trusted associate. Carried too far, a business can become an almost valueless shell of when it was a vibrant operating business if bad management or mismanagement covers up an inept course of action.

Whoever becomes a trusted manager, make sure you ask questions, monitor results, require accountability, and compensate for growth and improvement in all aspects of the business. Set agreed-upon measurable objectives for achievement and compensate on the basis of accomplishment of measurable objectives.

When deadlines are missed, when appointments are forgotten, or when important functions are overlooked, discussion of substance must be held. Persistent errors or evidence of weak or improper management should be cause for exit and replacement of the manager.

Chapter 35

EXIT STRATEGY II (PASSING THE BUSINESS TO A FAMILY MEMBER)

Passing along the business to a family member is a noble act, but don't allow nobility to be overwhelmed by unreasonable risk.

Let's say you want to pass along ownership as well as management to others. Start with the characteristics that will provide the greatest reward for the seller(s). Here are some considerations:

1. Your company is at the apex of company performance, financial, operations, sales revenue, net profit, stable workforce, established customers, and reliable suppliers.
2. Modest growth in company sales and profits over the past couple years.
3. You enjoy Friday afternoons more than you do Monday mornings.
4. You want to achieve new goals: reducing your golf score, fishing in Wyoming, skiing in Aspen, a trip to Australia.
5. Someone in your family and/or in your company is ready to assume the reins of company leadership and operation.
6. You have noticed personal tiredness, shortness of breath, or other potential lethal or casual health issues lately.

If you decide to transfer ownership to a family member, observe an important rule. Make sure you place no more retirement assets at risk than you can afford to lose. While you love your relative, you will never know how successful the proud new owner will be until they increase the company bottom-line profit on a consistent basis.

Be sure to be available for consultation for at least six months to the new owner. You don't need to micromanage the new owner, but your wise counsel can prevent losses that could be otherwise incurred.

It is easy to evaluate the person that takes over the business. Simply look at two things: (1) the bottom line (profit); and (2) trends (sales revenue↑, costs and expenses↓, and profits↑).

Recognize the risk of passing along a business to an uninspired relative with little experience.

Chapter 36

EXPENSE ACCOUNTS

Expense accounts should not be a form of income; that's what salaries and wages are for.

Most salesmen and women, as well as technicians and others whose jobs depend on travel and the incurring of travel and work-related expenses, spend money wisely. In spite of this assumed integrity and honesty, expense accounts should be monitored at all times.

The persons checking expense claims should use common sense and logic regarding miles traveled, cost of meals, and entertainment. Those who enhance their expense accounts often enter repetitive information that, when tracked by audits, can find the mendacious entries and trends.

Dishonesty is not an attribute of high performance of any employee.

Chapter 37

FINANCIAL STATEMENTS

The balance sheet is the report card showing the level of success in building wealth through creation of value.

Each month, a business should produce a balance sheet and a profit and loss statement. In addition, it is often helpful to compose a statement of cash flows. If you have a generic software package like QuickBooks, statements can be produced by your bookkeeper or accounting department.

The balance sheet is a status report of your financial condition at a point in time. The balance sheet is one of the principal documents that lending institutions refer to in determining credit risk. The value of a business is determined heavily by data taken from the balance sheet. Two ratios of importance to lenders and vendors are the current (or quick) ratio and the other is the debt ratio.

Current ratio is simply current assets divided by current liabilities. If the answer is over one, the company is considered liquid or solvent. If, on the other hand, the answer is less than 100 percent, your risk is increased. Usually, a company with current liabilities greater than current assets is slow-paying suppliers and unable to take discounts. The company may also be suffering from low sales resulting in poor cash flow.

Debt ratio is total liabilities divided by total assets. This number should be less than 100 percent indicating that the company has more total assets than total liabilities and is thus a solvent, going concern. If, however, the total liabilities are greater than total assets, the company is considered "under water" or insolvent.

Some businesses operate for long periods of time while insolvent. In the long run, a business must remain solvent to flourish.

The *profit and loss* statement is a record of sales, expenses, and profit over a specific period of time, such as a month, a quarter, or a year. Components of the profit and loss are sales, cost of goods sold (COGS) usually consisting of labor and materials, gross profit (sales minus COGS), expenses (mostly fixed expenses), and profit (before income taxes). See Chapter 26, Costs and Expenses.

COGS consists of variable expenses of labor and material; the more sales activity, the more labor and materials are used.

A third financial report that is useful is the cash flow statement or statement of cash flows. This report is designed to inform management regarding the amount of money received and spent. The cash flow statement is a report for a specific period of time and includes only cash actually received, ignoring accruals of debt or receipts. For example, the cash flow statement does not record depreciation since depreciation is a noncash expense (benefit). Cash flow statements that show positive cash flow generally reflect profitability of the business from increasing sales with favorable margins.

Chapter 38

FIRING EMPLOYEES

Departed employees should make room for improvements in staffing.

Before separating an employee, make sure that he or she has been advised that their performance does not meet company expectations and standards. Do everything possible to assist the underperforming worker to succeed. When a worker has been warned and continues to be unable to meet company requirements, it is time to separate that person from the company.

Never make the separation or "firing" a review of performance. Such discussions usually lead to unnecessary debate and confusing, conflicting remarks. Telling a person to leave the company is a command decision based on lack of performance by the employee as perceived by a company official.

An appropriate method of separating an employee for inability to perform to company standards is to simply tell the employee that the person's skills and abilities are a mismatch for the needs of the company. For these reasons, the person is being separated from employment at the company. "We wish you well and hope you have success in a new job. Thanks for your efforts in our behalf."

It is helpful to explain any benefits the employee has accrued, how to file for unemployment in the event that a new job is not available. It is also helpful to mention that the company name may be used on future job applications with a description of the responsibilities that the employee was involved with. Explain that their final paycheck will be mailed to their home address.

If the employee has violated a stated company policy and is separated for cause, the exit from company employment is simply to explain the violation and guide the former employee from company premises.

No matter what objections the employee may raise, the time is long past for arguments or disagreements. Simply escort the separated employee to the nearest entrance without words of criticism or derision. Make sure all details of the separation are written in the worker's personnel manual.

Chapter 39

GROWTH

Slow growth begets a listless workforce; fast growth strains funding;
optimum growth is planned.

There is that constant urge to "grow" your company. That's a good trait. However, there is the possibility of growth that can be too fast as well as growth that is too slow. Here are some rules of thumb or guidelines:

For most companies with varying margins should try to grow in the range of about 5 percent annually. Here's why: inflation, also known as COLA (cost of living adjustment), or CPI (consumer price index), varies from year to year from about 2 percent to 4 percent. If your company increases in sales revenue and profit by about 5 percent, your company is exceeding the inflation rate by a small margin.

If your company generates sales and profits of less than the annual inflation rate, the company is actually shrinking slightly. If the trend continues year after year, the company is at risk of becoming a has-been or insolvent firm based on slumping financial and operating performance.

If your company achieves growth at 10 percent or even 15 percent in a year, it sounds good; but generally, that company will incur additional debt. Sometimes that debt is a burden that suppresses profit and may affect credit ratings by delinquent supplier remittances and current and long-term debt payments.

Budget growth and the cash flow and capital that is required to finance that growth. Before borrowing to finance growth, evaluate risk and make sure the economic equation has a positive result.

Annual growth compounded at 5 percent will mean a company will increase by 28.3 percent in five years.
Annual growth of 7 percent will yield an increase of 41.8 percent in five years.
Annual growth of 9 percent will yield an increase of 56.6 percent in five years.
Remember the seven and ten rule. At 7 percent return, investments will about double in ten years.
At 10 percent return, investments will approximately double in seven years.

Chapter 40

HARASSMENT

Truth: Never laugh at harassment; it is not funny!

Harassment in any form is repulsive and must be eliminated instantly when discovered. One of the most viral forms of harassment is sexual in nature. Sexual harassment often occurs when an employee makes lewd comments, stares at certain physical characteristics, or touches another person inappropriately.

Other forms of harassment are bullying because of appearance such as long or colored hair, tattoos, nose or lip rings, overweight, underweight, choice of clothing, or general appearance. Harassment also is a morale chaser and should be crushed on the first evidence of violation. Harassment of anyone in any form—physical, verbal, Internet, or written (fellow employees, customers, suppliers, shoppers) or that may be suspected of being gay, lesbian, bisexual, or transgender (LGBT)—must be absolutely prohibited.

Another form of harassment comes from people who may taunt other workers at a level different than theirs. The source of the harassment may be the result of jealousy or simply contempt for other individuals in other departments.

The company should have an effective, confidential reporting and follow-up system to verify claims of any form of harassment. When it is determined the name(s) of the violator(s), the person(s) should be disciplined immediately. If the discipline does not include dismissal for cause, the penalty for anyone who is a repeat offender should include separation from the company with forfeiture of benefits.

The entire company benefits when employee/partners that violate common sense rules of behavior are eliminated from the company payroll. Harassment in all its iterations is intolerable in a workplace.

Chapter 41

HEALTH

An ounce of prevention is worth a pound of cure.

At latest report, health care consumes about 17 percent of the national budget. When considering spending by individuals, the cost may be greater. We feel better when we are healthy; we work more efficiently when we are feeling good. Serious illness is both expensive and time-consuming.

As owner, manager, or other company official, healthy on-the-job presence is important. It is equally important that workers spend all possible workdays fulfilling their assignments.

It is wise to undergo an annual physical checkup during early and middle years of ownership and management. As we grow older, it is appropriate to accelerate checkups and submit to appropriate diagnostic tests.

It is important that workers and their families are covered with health insurance on their own, through the employer, or through government plans and mandates.

If an on-the-job injury results in a flesh wound, have a treatment kit handy for bandages and disinfectants. If your company presents risks of dust or flying particles, have an eyewash fountain nearby. Provide ear, vision, and other preventative equipment. See Chapter 1, Accidents; and Chapter 78, Safety.

Employees who exhibit signs of flu or other illness that may be communicable might serve the company's best interests by staying home during the most contagious days of their disorder.

Budget the planned cost of health insurance to cover the rapidly-increasing costs of healthcare.

Chapter 42

HIRING EMPLOYEES

A good employee is an asset; an inept employee is an expense.

When considering a prospect for employment, ask about reasons for departure from previous jobs. If remarks are made such as, "couldn't get along with the boss" or "the foreman had it in for me," the applicant may have an attitude problem. Always try to determine what the applicant was doing where long gaps in employment are noted.

Perhaps most important in the initial interview(s) with prospective employees is a complete explanation of what is expected in the position under consideration. Make sure that the job expectations are clearly understood.

When the job is a full-time position, assure the prospect that he or she will be reviewed in thirty days, sixty days, or ninety days. Assure them that they will receive an increase after ninety days if their performance meets company standards as outlined in the interview.

Always give applicants hope of both increased responsibility and earnings. Be absolutely realistic and never make promises about increased wages or responsibilities unless the statements reflect the high probability of what may happen in the future.

Be sure to avoid disqualifying any applicant for reasons of age, handicap status, gender, sexual orientation, race, religion, or ethnicity. If your company has an appearance standard or a "dress code," make sure such a requirement is reasonable.

See Appendix H, Employee Application Form

Chapter 43

HONESTY

Proverb: A liar has to have a good memory.

Honesty is the best policy. This is an old axiom, and it is as true today as it was when someone said it for the first time a long time ago.

You must expect honesty from your employees to have a successful company. Your accountant must never "cook the books." Your purchasing agent or manager must always admit if he forgot to order product on time. Your inventory counters must always turn in correct counts every time. Your sales people must always explain the precise reasons why a customer stopped buying. There are myriads of cases of inaccurate communications that have been troubling for governments and companies.

The way you affirm honest and complete communications is to be absolutely honest in all communications and dealings. This applies to supervisors as well as managers, officers, and company owners.

It is better to remain silent than tell a lie.

Chapter 44

INCENTIVE COMPENSATION

Employee compensation must always be measured by each person's contribution to company output.

Every employee should have an incentive (beyond payroll) to do an outstanding job in quality excellence, high productivity, and safety and do all this with a good attitude toward the company and their job. Average performance is payroll; superior performance is rewarded.

Workers appreciate a pat on the back, but they also appreciate a little addition to their back pocket or purse. Here are some ideas:

Take 20 percent of company net profit and make a "pool" of funds for distribution monthly based on forty-hour earnings (without overtime) and salaries. To encourage teamwork, make everyone in the company a party to the distributions. If you have commission sales people, they should be exempt from the plan.

Let's say company profit for April was $10,000. Twenty percent of the total is $2,000. Let's say that payroll for April was $50,000. Judy's salary for the month was $2,500 or 5 percent of the total payroll, so she would receive 5 percent of the "pool" of funds or $100.

Some forfeitures should be considered. Anyone who had an accident during that month forfeits their bonus share for that month. Persons who had unexcused absences during the month should not participate.

On the positive side, it could be worthy to also offer special compensation for perfect attendance or other outstanding achievements by workers.

Companies who have active equitable incentive plans usually more than pay for the cost of the bonuses by additional savings in materials, labor, and enthusiasm for work.

Chapter 45

INNOVATION

"If you are too busy to get your job done, figure out a better way to do it."

Innovation is a thoughtful process of improving procedures or ideas that are accepted as routine standards. History indicates that the bicycle was invented in about 1800. It is reported that it was made from wood: wood wheels, frame, and seat. It had no pedals, and thus the "rider" simply used legs and feet to make the "vehicle" move forward or backward. Over the centuries, innovators have added handlebars, pedals, metal frames, and a wide number of gear choices. In addition, bicycles now are equipped with lights, horns, bottle holders, baggage racks, and other accessories.

If allowed to think from a blank sheet of paper, you and your employees can create interesting and profitable methods of improving the activities and products of your company. The secret is—it's really no secret—that company leadership must encourage innovation by being results-oriented and allow all employees the opportunity to create. Innovation is often the opposite of "this is the way we have always done it." The rewards for innovation throughout a company are huge.

Innovative changes recommended and implemented should be rewarded by at least recognition and most often with an award of money or something of value (theater tickets, book, a trip, or a gift card). Encourage innovation and creativity; reward it!

Chapter 46

INSURANCE

Insurance isn't needed until you need it.

Insurance should be purchased and maintained for virtually every hazard that is possible or probable. Some agencies deal in many of the insurance categories, while some are more specific to areas of insurance. Get the best rates from the best companies and get competitive quotes annually. Read the details and provisions of all policies and have the sales person explain all details of coverage, limitations, procedures, and net cost of premiums. Because each state has its own insurance provisions, this chapter only covers guidelines. Some categories of insurance are:

Life insurance, especially on person(s) who are invested in the company, especially principal stockholders who are also company officials. This can be "term life" or other forms of coverage. The lowest cost and usually the most useful insurance covers the life of the owner and other family members and possibly company officials. It is usually inappropriate to have life insurance entwined with investment features. Beneficiaries should be family members, although banks will often insist on assignment of insurance payouts when unusual risk is present.

Liability and property (buildings, contents, vehicles, accidents, fire, wind and storm, i.e., all hazards and casualties)
Workers' compensation (State mandated; injury, disability short term, long term)
Health
Life
Dental
Specific (cancer, others)

In general, workers' compensation insurance rates are set by the state depending on your company's accident and injury experience rating. Accidents and injuries are expensive; have your insurance carrier hold safety meetings frequently regarding forklift operation, wearing safety devices (glasses, ear protection, hard hats, gloves, dust masks, and breathing apparatus). If your company uses or sells toxic gases, you may need evaluation of respirators. See Chapter 1, Accidents.

Keep an insurance calendar so that expiration and renewal dates are always observed. Never allow any insurance coverage to lapse because of the risk of loss or damage even over a short period of no coverage.

Evaluate insurance coverage annually to make sure all reasonable hazards are adequately covered.

Chapter 47

INTEREST

Earned interest contributes to profit; interest paid is an expense item.

The two most important sources of interest are the interest paid out and the interest earned. Rates of interest income or outflow may be from 1 percent or 2 percent and as much as almost 30 percent. A company that borrows on a credit line, mortgage, or promissory note in the amount of $100,000 may pay as little as a couple of thousand dollars in interest. However, the company that finds itself without conventional sources of capital may be stuck with paying 29 percent on credit card credit extensions to the tune of $10,000 or more on credit card debt when used as capital acquisition.

Interest can play an important role in delinquent receivables. If your state allows late fees or interest of 2 percent per month for delinquent accounts, the annual percentage rate climbs to 24 percent. In spite of the high income potential of receivable interest, it is always better to collect receivables on time, every time if possible. The reason is that money received from current receivables can be put to work paying other bills that often earn cash discounts.

While business managers should not be intimidated by interest costs, it is prudent to always budget for interest income and interest costs. Remember that all amounts are cumulative, and note that money invested at 10 percent will approximately double in seven years. And money invested at 7 percent will approximately double in ten years.

Keep in mind that if your company has interest bearing promissory notes on a couple of hundred thousand dollars in machinery and equipment, a credit line for inventory and accounts receivable, plus a sizeable mortgage on real estate, interest is an expense to be reckoned with.

Chapter 48

INVENTORY

JIT is a balancing act

Inventory should be taken frequently, preferably every month. Some companies utilize perpetual inventory and eliminate a regular physical count. While this may be efficient, it allows unintended changes to take place. For example, a computer clerk could enter a data entry incorrectly. It is possible that shipments and deliveries could be incorrectly recorded. In some cases, inventory items can become soiled or damaged or obsolete. In a worst case, there could be an employee that has a predisposition to liberate something for personal gain.

To avoid the possibility of inventory shrinkage from taking place, a monthly count is preferable. However, if this is too awkward or expensive, try this solution and make a lesser number of counts per year. Take a physical inventory count when the last day of the month falls on a Friday, Saturday, or Sunday. By doing this, there will be the least interruption to normal business hours even if your business stays open on Saturdays and/or Sundays.

Inventory turns is an important ratio that reveals how much money is invested in inventory. The "trick" regarding inventory control is to utilize as much as possible the concept of JIT (Just-in-Time). Unit quantity purchasing, shipping, unit quantity pricing, supplier payment terms, number of suppliers, supplier lead times, rate of utilization, shelf life, storage capacity, and obsolescence are all critical factors in determining buying and storing decisions.

When the company is overstocked, cash flow is negatively affected because available cash for liquidating debt is extended. When the company has a shortage of inventory, company production, or service may be slowed that in turn affects accounts receivable and cash flow.

The higher the number of inventory turns, the more efficient is your inventory investment. Inventory control is the fine art of avoiding shortages and back orders while maintaining the lowest possible investment in inventory to avoid obsolescence, inordinate investment expense, and damage.

See Appendix C, Inventory Turns

Chapter 49

JOB DESCRIPTIONS

Something is wrong if you are always right.

Although this chapter is entitled "Job Descriptions," the expression is outdated. One of the principal reasons that it is no longer an accurate outline of individual or group specific duties in that it reflects as many limitations as opportunities. Thus, the expression that may be more appropriate is "Expectations." Instead of being a summary written up by management, it is a document that is crafted by both supervisor and worker/partner.

Expectations should be a complete list of what the company needs to have done by the employee partner. The list of expectations should be results-oriented and should have a timetable for completion. There should be a schedule of anticipated rate of progress toward the goal of greater responsibility and/or increased compensation along with constantly increasing productivity.

See Appendix H, Employee Application Form

Chapter 50

LAGNIAPPE (A LITTLE EXTRA)

What we should have done is now irrelevant; what we must do now is important.

This is a word that is used in Louisiana that has both Spanish and French (Creole) roots. It means a "little extra," a gift, or a bonus. The word can also refer to "profit sharing" for employees.

If an employee is well paid, why do you need "lagniappe" or something a little extra, e.g., profit sharing? Ask yourself this question: if you worked especially hard to help your company achieve higher goals, would you appreciate receiving a little extra in your paycheck? Of course you would because it is a means of expressing appreciation for superior service.

Your company should employ people who understand superior service. Morale can be built and sustained by celebrating achievements large and small. Although certificates of achievement and congratulatory comments are valuable, probably nothing sways the dedication of an employee more than money in exchange for and recognition of superior performance.

Something "a little extra" also applies to customers. Do you remember the little extra gift that a salesman presented to you when you purchased a car or a refrigerator? Upon completion of a project or service, if you are able to explain the special gift of service or product, it will be remembered.

The point to remember is that lagniappe is not about average people doing an average job; it is about dedicated people doing a superior job.

See Chapter 44, Incentive Compensation.

Chapter 51

LUCK

The smarter I work, the luckier I get!

Luck plays a role in every business (and personal) decision, but don't depend on it. The better planning that is done at your company and the more attention that is paid to productivity, safety, quality, and attitude, the luckier you will get.

Luck is time and place. Never forget that. Luck is time and place. You must intersect time and place with your ability to be there on time, every time. Luck is an accumulation of good decisions. Good decisions are the result of logical good sense in planning, execution, and follow-up. Your decisions won't be correct every time, but you must improve your "batting average" by paying attention to the reasons bad decisions have been made in the past. Mistakes are great teachers.

Luck may also be defined as the intersection of time, place, and probability.

Chapter 52

MANAGEMENT

Self-management is accountability. Managing a process is logic and common sense. Managing others is a rewarding profession.

When managers accept their positions, they are accepting the challenge of meeting goals and achieving certain results within an agreed-upon time frame. The difference between managers and hourly workers is that hourly workers are exchanging their skills for an hourly wage. The job of managers or supervisors is to inspire their employees to help them achieve timely goals. Hourly workers leave work when their shift ends. Managers leave work when their objective is achieved.

The three key steps to good management are:

1. Management of self: setting priorities, gaining and applying knowledge, goal setting and achievement, on-time completion every time with quality. Examples of management positions that achieve personal goals are architecture, artistic performance (painting, needle crafts, sculpture, music etc.).

2. Management of machinery, equipment, and environment; examples include machine operators, truck drivers, etc. For example, a truck driver that has driven a couple of million miles without an accident is an achiever in his occupational category.

3. Management of other people: the highest achievement in management is the person that can maximize output of other workers through careful planning, execution, and follow-up. Top managers are excellent communicators and leave no doubt about the goals to be achieved and

how to reach them. Top managers are results-oriented and usually leave the process to those who do the work and get the job done through innovation and creative thought.

The best supervisor/manager is one who achieves objectives through people who believe that successful on-time completion of objectives was their own idea to begin with.

Chapter 53

MARKETING

Markets are fickle and mutate constantly; products and services must be adaptable to meet rapid changes.

Marketing is the link between product availability and sales at all levels. Market specialists must be creative regarding displays, samples, signs, brochures, advertising, and all the elements that help transform shoppers into buyers.

In order to be successful in their quest of dominating a market, market specialists and their sales counterparts must constantly be on the lookout for trends, pricing changes, technology upgrades, new market entries, revised competitive offerings, and changes in logistics. In marketing, logistics refers to instantaneous delivery and all levels of availability of purchases by individuals, companies, and others. U.S. Mail, FedEx, UPS, and other modes of delivery are getting items from source to recipient faster than ever. Drone delivery and other fast methods are now in use and will certainly be growing. The big equation to solve is the balance between speed and cost.

Marketers have a plethora of choices to do market research to fit their products and services to their geographic and economic end-use customers. By using a variety of market investigation services (in-house and outsourced), companies can have a profile of demand and respond by employing sales techniques, pricing, and programs to amplify sales.

Keep sharp awareness of market trends!

Chapter 54

MEDIOCRITY

Mediocrity has a purpose; it is a standard for those who find excellence out of reach.

Mediocrity is an infectious disease of companies that are undisciplined and allow people to dress down to low standards of appearance and supervisors who accept "good enough" as a standard of output.

Every person in every department should demand excellence from themselves and others. Employees willing to accept poor quality of service or products must be weeded out in humane fashion so they can have opportunities with companies with lower standards.

Excellence in pursuit of perfection is the name of the game of success.

Chapter 55

MEETINGS

Bad joke: *Sales are down 23 percent, but meetings are up 30 percent!*

Meetings are an essential tool in leadership and management. Meetings with groups and individuals can be very productive in planning, sales, marketing, administration, operations, personnel reviews, financial management, and a host of other purposes.

Here are some important rules for effective meetings:

1. Always inform all attendees of the topics to be discussed: the date, the starting time, the time of adjournment, and the results expected.
2. Make sure all those invited to a meeting are or will be involved in one or more of the topics to be discussed. Wasting the time of spectators is wasting the time of everyone.
3. Meeting coordinator should never *(never)* be late and should expect all attendees to be there on time and prepared to discuss the previously planned topics.
4. Do *not* allow any conversations to stray from the topics selected for discussion.
5. *Never* allow anyone to raise his or her voice or scream.
6. Turn off cell phones and decline taking any phone calls (except emergencies).
7. If the meeting business is not complete and needs to extend beyond the stated time for adjournment, state the revised time for adjournment and end it as stated.

8.   If the meeting results in task assignments for attendees, write down the assignments and the date for completion of the task.

9.   Follow up on all task assignments as a result of the meeting (never fail).

Meetings may be held electronically. If so, all the rules above still apply.

When meeting with an employee, it is often preferable to meet in their office or venue rather than yours. Employees usually feel more comfortable in his/her turf and may be more likely to contribute to the meeting agenda more freely.

Meetings can and should be brief and frequent. Speak about predetermined topics and always take a few minutes for questions. Answer questions honestly and completely. If you do not have an answer to a question, promise a response at a defined later date and make good on the date and the response.

Chapter 56

MISSION STATEMENT

It is folly to embark on a voyage without compass, map, and confidence in mast, sails, and rudder.

Always develop a mission statement to apply to your business. The mission statement becomes a beacon, a rudder that will direct thoughts and actions throughout the life of the company.

Mission statements should be thoughtful and brief. For example, many police departments have what may be their mission statements on their vehicles that read, "To protect and to serve."

Microsoft's mission statement for 2015 was listed as follows: "Empower every person and every organization on the planet to achieve more."

Mission statements should have words about customer service, honesty, integrity, and words of comfort and satisfaction.

Here is a sample: "The ABCD Company is committed to long-term customer satisfaction through quality products delivered and installed on time by highly skilled employees."

Another: "Our Company stands behind our products and services to the complete satisfaction of our customers. Founded in 1975, our people and our products are second to none. We guarantee it!"

Your mission statement should appear in many places for all to see and be constantly reminded of company core values and objectives. Mission statements are ideally ten to thirty-five words, always in clear print and located on brochures, displays, and in high-traffic locations.

Mission statements have no value in a file drawer or in the desk of a big shot.

Chapter 57

NEPOTISM

Those who underestimate others often overestimate themselves.

It seems silly that some companies don't allow close relatives to work in the same department or the same company. Every employee must have a strong work ethic and must behave in a business-like manner at all times when at work. While conspiracies occasionally develop among workers, most employees, when motivated and inspired, are most likely to be honest and diligent on behalf of the company.

There are even some advantages to nepotism. If Joe has been a good productive employee for the company for three years and recommends his cousin, Charles, there is a good probability that the cousin is a good worker. Of course if he isn't, you suggest he works elsewhere and show him the door.

In the event you are worried that two relatives working in the same department could conspire to steal or embezzle, sign each other's time cards or other violations of company policy, simply warn them to avoid these violations. When the violations are observed and confirmed, these conspirators should be separated for cause.

It is worthwhile to consider a "bounty" for any employee who recommends employment for a friend or a relative that turns out to be a good worker. If such a program is developed, the reward should be presented after a period of time of satisfactory performance of at least ninety days by the new employee partner.

Chapter 58

NETWORKING

Networking opens avenues of information and trends at all levels;
it must never be used for illegal price setting or unethical behavior.

One of the most important pursuits for business people to accommodate is networking. Carried on effectively both socially and in business associations, networking can net considerable knowledge of new ideas, new products, additional sales opportunities, and contacts with banks, attorneys, accountants, and others that can be great sources for enhanced learning.

An example is attendance at an annual convention or conference of business leaders in your industry or in your region. You should always be on the lookout for other men and women whose businesses are similar to yours in one way or another and exchange various forms of information. After leaving the event, it is sometimes worthwhile to exchange information throughout the year.

A visit to your nearest community college will almost always turn up a course that you or some of your employees can take at low cost to sharpen knowledge and skills. Since you have met some folks in the classroom and in the administration building, you can often find sources for hiring new and well-trained workers.

Networking with customers at the annual trade show or home and garden event will almost always end up with at least several leads regarding potential customers. As a courtesy, it is often helpful to send some employees to the show or exhibit also for networking.

Networking can be accomplished to some degree by joining a local service club, the country club, the chamber of commerce, or Better Business Bureau. Data and people in these organizations can often provide useful information and guidance.

Here are a couple cautionary notes. When you attend a distant convention that combines social contacts along with business ones, strive to spend your time in caucuses, lectures, and seminars that can yield valuable ideas. Avoid the habit of going to expensive conventions simply to shake hands and talk about the weather.

Be careful to avoid conversing with competitors or suppliers about pricing that could be interpreted as illegal "price fixing." The penalties are rather stiff for those business people that deliberately conspire to establish parity "fixed" pricing for customers.

Chapter 59

NEWSLETTER

Noteworthy: Employees and their families love to read about and see photos of themselves and their workplace.

A company newsletter used to be called an Internal Organ. That sounds more like a kidney or stomach or liver, so my preference is the word *Newsletter*. This is an often-overlooked important link in the employment relationship. It can be published weekly, monthly, or even quarterly. I strongly recommend at least a monthly newsletter for all employees. Publish pictures of "person of the month" or members of a winning team (bowling, softball—you get the idea). New employees appreciate seeing their photo with a little background bio in the monthly newsletter.

The company newsletter is the perfect medium for announcing new products, policies, and other important company news. The newsletter is an excellent place to publish stories of satisfied customers.

While there may be no visible benefit for having a periodic newsletter, it tends to increase morale. And you can bet that anyone whose photo appears in the current issue takes it home to show family and friends.

Chapter 60

OBSOLESCENCE

Warning: Expedite the disposal of obsolete products and processes.

When a new business is established, the opening features fresh displays, clean floors, walls, and ceilings. If the company sells merchandise of any kind, all items are fresh and new usually in attractive packaging.

After even a short time in business, some items will fall into obsolescence. This is especially true with electronic products and other sale articles that are dependent on changing technology.

When any item or service is being replaced with a newer product or service, get rid of the obsolete items quickly! Sell them at cost or below cost; sometimes you can even give them away just to make room for new replacement products. Don't "romance" certain special items by keeping them long after they have been superseded with new, exciting replacements.

If obsolete products find repose in a back corner of a warehouse, make sure they appear on inventory report at a token value such as $1. This will keep pressure on to make sure the items will be removed from taking up space.

Chapter 61

ORGANIZATION

Regardless of size, all businesses should constantly strive to increase
both financial and intrinsic value of the enterprise.

When forming your company, there are several choices of organizational styles to consider.

The simplest form of organization is a "sole proprietorship." Many to most small businesses employ this style for reasons of simplicity. It is easy and inexpensive to create; it is generally only lightly regulated by local, state, and federal rules and statutes, and income taxes are paid based on the earnings of the sole proprietor.

Partnerships may be "ships" that rock and roll in a sea of dissention among partners that were friends on the day of organization but insist on different methods of achieving success. On the day the enterprise is formed, the partners should create a buy/sell agreement that describes the precise terms of payment by the departing partner to the remaining partners. This document must be forward-looking to account for added or diminished company value during the partnership period. The buy/sell value should be based on the financial share of company ownership on the date of "buy" or "sell." Both proprietorships and partnerships may have difficulty in raising capital because of the sometimes limited assets available for collateral or pledging against loans and credit accommodations. Also, in both proprietorships and partnerships, participants can lose more than their investment

Corporations are legal entities created and regulated at the state level. Often called the 'C' corporation, this organizational style usually has a stock issue at par (often $1), has a charter; losses are limited to amount invested, and the bad news is that corporate organizations are subject to double taxation. This means that the enterprise is taxed on earnings, and dividends (share of profits) are also taxed when distributed to shareholders.

Another form of corporate structure is referred to a "subchapter S" that allows the corporate profits to be mingled with dividend distributions.

Some companies are formed as limited liability companies (LLC). In this organizational form, risk of investment may be high but investing partners can only lose the maximum of their investment.

Warning: It is highly recommended that if you are planning to invest several thousand dollars as startup capital for any business that you seek the advice and counsel of an attorney regarding the complexities of filing government information, creating a charter, appointing directors (who may have legal liability in case of bankruptcy), establishing charter stock and other vicissitudes when forming a company. An attorney can help create documents and policies that can prevent difficulties later on.

Chapter 62

PEOPLE

Employees are every company's most valuable asset but also its highest expense.

The most valuable asset of every company is its people. When that is clearly understood, your company will have the best people available to sell and ship products and services that enjoy increasing demand.

Respect all people regardless of race, gender, age, religion, ethnicity, and handicap status and provide inspiration for perfection.

Employees that show the spark of excellence should be appreciated while those who are untrained must be trained, and those that make repetitive mistakes and errors and don't fit the culture of competence should be working elsewhere.

All companies develop a culture, a standard operating procedure of discipline, courtesy, honesty, results orientation, timeliness, meeting deadlines, respect for others, and confidence based on training, skill, and experience. Define the culture of your company and review various aspects that are working well while other qualities of behavior may get out of sync with company principles. Unhappy employees can spread venom to others and pull down morale and productivity.

When you buy a brick or board, you know exactly what you are getting; when hiring an employee, you find out what you got days, weeks, months, and years later.

Chapter 63

PERSONNEL REVIEWS

When everybody is somebody, nobody is anybody.

Each employee partner should be reviewed both periodically (such as twice a year) or at the culmination of an event. The annual or semiannual review is an accumulation of comments in the personnel file regarding achievements, disciplinary actions, absences, tardiness, and supervisory recommendations.

When a specific event takes place such as a serious accident, costly error, or an achievement above and beyond the call of duty that is a good time to have a heart-to-heart discussion with the employee/partner. If the event was a positive achievement, tell the employee how pleased you are and put the employee/partner's picture and some commentary in the company newsletter.

When the review is negative, outline precisely the faults and failings that have been observed. Ask the employee if he or she is willing to try to improve performance. Discuss what actions and changes in behavior that are planned. Establish a thirty- to ninety-day term for improvement and follow up. In the event there are no improvements or only limited changes, you may want to give another chance to the employee or replace them promptly.

Employee reviews should be the most fulfilling task that all leaders in the company should relish doing. When an employee is brought in for review, there are three basic rules to make the discussion most dynamic and useful.

The first step should always be a question to the employee regarding his or her view of their job. You should ask questions about the ways they are supervised and the way they supervise. The best supervisors always have the best interest of the employee and the company.

Next, the supervisor should reveal his or her perception of the job the employee is doing. This should include statements of criticism and compliment. Include dialogue regarding suggestions for improvement in some areas while maintaining high performance in the area where excellence is already observed.

Finally, agreement must be reached on objectives and chronology; objectives should be measurable, and time for achievement should be weeks or months ahead. If the timetable for achievement is more than six months in advance, an interim meeting should be planned to evaluate progress toward agreed-upon goals.

Employees are the most valuable asset of any enterprise.

See Chapter 62, People; and Appendix G, Employee Review Form.

Chapter 64

POLITICS

We have the best Congress money can buy. – Will Rogers

Political discussions are strictly optional in the business setting. It seems reasonable that employers should resist the temptation to influence voting among employees. The political system in the United States does seem to command a lot of time, energy, and money, especially during the seemingly endless campaign seasons. However, signs posted on business property may be inviting to some prospects and customers while repelling other possible patrons. This is strictly a personal decision with the question: "Do you want to please some customers at the expense of discouraging others?" Another question is if you plaster even a few signs, banners, or other political posters on your property, you may simply trigger time-wasting debates among employees.

That does not mean that you should not support your favorite candidate. You must be the judge of how much energy you want to use to influence others to vote for your candidate. One important point is that usually, it is favorable for employers to encourage employees to vote, regardless of who their favorite candidate may be.

Chapter 65

PRIORITIES

*A priority worthy of mention is to fasten your seatbelts before the
vehicle moves.*

It is highly probable that some to most leaders establish priorities in their mind
or on paper as a natural activity to make sure all things get done . . . on time.
However, there are people in leadership roles that don't set priorities and are late
for meetings, file their taxes on an extended schedule, and sometimes even miss
important appointments and deadlines.

There is no excuse for not prioritizing activities by aligning activities in your
mind or on a piece of paper.

No matter how difficult it may be, there are many ways of establishing priorities
for the conduct of business and personal activities. Require the discipline of
prioritizing activities among your employees and practice it emphatically yourself.

There is a triumph in priorities.

Chapter 66

PROBLEM SOLVING

Convert problems to opportunities.

When a business is created and the founder(s) jump through all the hoops of organization, capitalization, staffing, and filing all the local, state, and federal licensing and corporate requirements, it is easy to fall prey to the concept that the founders have all the answers. Nothing could be further from the truth, especially if wisdom has prevailed, and many of the employees are competent thinkers, planners, and performers.

Adjusting to life in a hierarchy or young bureaucracy, allow employees to help solve problems through their own creativity. One of the best approaches to assuring that this will happen is to respond positively to workers who bring questions to be answered by the all-knowing, all-wise company founder. When asked for a simple answer to a dilemma related by the supervisor, secretary, or other employee, ask the inquirer what they think might be the best answer to their question. Pause and allow time for the person to rotate a possible answer over in his/her mind.

When a response is issued, consider alternatives and select what seems to be the best solution in concert with the employee. Build confidence in employees at all levels. It is usually true that decisions in an organization, some of the best ideas and decisions come from the lowest level of the company hierarchy. What is often typical is that supervisors (bosses) discount the thoughts and ideas of lower-level workers out of hand. Following a "no-confidence" vote, workers may tend to withhold good ideas and suggestions.

Don't ever forget that employees are both the company's greatest asset and its greatest expense.

Don't waste both assets and expenses.

Chapter 67

PROCRASTINATION

Bad looks good when worse happens.

Experience has taught us that procrastination, the philosophy of putting off decisions and actions, has been more destructive than almost any other violation of good management and leadership.

Here's an approach to decision making and taking action. Decide on a time and date in the future when logic dictates that it will be too late to achieve an objective resulting from enacting the decision. Too late may mean taking advantage of a special price or product or service.

Suppose for example that you read in the newspaper that the introductory sale for a new model computer will be on Tuesday of next week. If today is Wednesday of the prior week, it is clear that you have until the store closes next Tuesday to make a decision. The penalty for procrastinating beyond Tuesday may be the $100 saving that could have been gained. In addition, the prospective buyer loses the benefits that would have been available by the purchase.

Good managers simply don't procrastinate; they don't put off important decisions. The risk is always ripe with regrets if action is postponed until the last minute or until it is too late completely. Procrastination usually has a cost, and that cost is that the procrastinator is in a position of weakness for negotiation and settlement.

Chapter 68

PRODUCTIVITY

Axiom: You can't manage what you can't measure.

Company output must be measured. All departments must be measured. All personnel must be measured. Productivity is one of the most important measures of success by people, departments, and the total company. Without high productivity, a company cannot thrive and grow.

What is productivity, and how is it measured? Productivity may have many definitions, but the one that is most useful is simply the output (sales, revenue, volume, billings, etc.) measured against input of labor cost (direct labor and/or total payroll). The method of calculation is as simple as the definition. Divide the total dollars of revenue for any period (hour, day, week, month, year) by the dollars of direct payroll or the dollars of total payroll for that period. The answer is productivity.

Examples: Sales for the month at Tom's Tool and Die, Incorporated amounted to $80,000. Total payroll for the month amounted to $19,700. Direct payroll was $14,200. (Direct payroll is the amount paid to all workers that had a direct role in producing company products: tools and dies.) As a result of the foregoing numbers, total productivity for the month was $80,000 divided by $19,700 is equal to $4.06, and direct productivity was $80,000 divided by $14,200 is equal to $5.63. Each dollar of payroll cost yielded $4.06 (total productivity) in sales revenue. Keep productivity trending higher.

Check with others in your industry to exchange productivity data and you can determine if your productivity meets "competitive" criteria and standards. Productivity is a great measure for establishing "benchmarking" or "best practices."

See Chapter 11, Best Practices.

Chapter 69

PROFIT

Top line is vanity; bottom line is sanity.

Philosophically, your business may have been formed to serve your fellow citizens or some other lofty goal. But the core objective of any business should be to generate a profit. The reason is simple; when entrepreneurs take the risk of investing capital, time, knowledge, and skill, they have a right to believe that a profit can be generated by serving their customers and other stakeholders.

Profit, but how much? The answer is based on your business plan that includes sales revenue, costs, expenses, margins, and all other financial activities of the firm.

The true test of profitability is by comparing forecast and actual profit performance with comparable investment. For example, if you have invested $1 million in inventory, equipment, and other expenditures, you should expect at least as much or more than could be received from these alternative investments in real estate or securities in the form of publicly traded stocks and/or bonds. Over the past few years, investment in securities has yielded returns of from 3 percent to 7 percent. Based on this measure, you should expect to produce at least that level of return from your investment in inventory and equipment. Some businesses plan for returns of 15 percent to account for investment risk, market risk, and outside economic influences.

All businesses are different, and economies are changing constantly, so profitability is a constant challenge. Here are some rules of thumb to consider:

•   Profit should be generated at least nine out of the twelve months of a calendar or fiscal year.

•   Breakeven should be calculated each month to determine what level of revenue is required for profitability (See Chapter 12, Breakeven).

•   Product categories produce varying net profit percentages; promote those with the highest margins and returns.

•   Get rid of products that are nearing expiration of shelf life or are getting close to obsolescence or have dents or scrapes. Carrying marginal products on inventory beyond their useful marketability is wasting time and money.

•   The ultimate goal of entrepreneurship is to accumulate value (net worth) on your balance sheet.

Chapter 70

PURCHASING

Savings, no matter how small, are cumulative.

Purchasing agents should be among the most talented positions in every company. These men and women who spend precious (sometimes scarce) company funds must be alert to a host of variables such as quantity pricing, delivery size, carriers (truck, UPS, FedEx, rail, lead times, ships/containers, Just-in-Time or JIT, specifications, and other considerations).

To encompass all these variables related to each order, the purchasing agent or department must be alert at all times to receiving on-time delivery, top quality without damage, lowest pricing available, and correct order size. This process is known as EOQ (economic order quantity) that embraces all the considerations of supplier lead times, delivery schedules, and rate of utilization after arrival.

Purchasing agents, because they make so many buying decisions, are often vulnerable to financial or other gift incentives by vendors to place orders with their company. That is a good reason why all purchasing agents (and their departments) should participate in an incentive plan that rewards good behavior as well as meeting the traditional requirements of best value pricing and on-time deliveries.

All ongoing supplier relationships should be reviewed and audited periodically to assure that the relationship is value-based, sound, and robust for both buyer and sellers.

Chapter 71

QUALITY

Quality is not optional; it dictates price, volume, customers and public perceptions.

As mentioned in the front of this book, quality is one of the core requirements for successful business operation and right up there with productivity, safety, and attitude.

Everybody in your company should be a "quality control supervisor." There should be no excuses for not having perfect quality. No employee should ever blame another for bad quality. Flaws and defects should be found and fixed before sale when defects become more expensive.

When flaws are discovered in product or service, it should be fixed immediately (or sooner).

Your company should always be the quality gold standard for all products in your market. Absolutely.

Chapter 72

RATIOS AND PERCENTAGES

Look and acknowledge trends in all activities.

To evaluate the changes in your company's financial stability, it is important to compute ratios and percentages each month. Here are some suggestions:

Balance Sheet: Current ratio. This is simply current assets divided by current liabilities. The answer should always be greater than 1 (or 100 percent) because that means the company is "liquid" and has more current assets than current liabilities. The current ratio is important because lending institutions and vendors (suppliers) use that information to help determine credit worthiness. It helps banks and other lenders determine how much debt can be incurred that may be liquidated over a period of time. The current ratio is used by suppliers to help determine how much purchasing your company can pay for within their payment terms.

Debt Ratio: This is a ratio of total liabilities divided by total assets. This ratio should always be less than 100 percent which means that total debt is less than total assets. This too is an important ratio for both lenders and suppliers so they can determine risk of loans, credit accommodations, and accounts payable your firm can deal with comfortably as related to all other debt obligations of your company.

Other important ratios include Day Sales Outstanding (DSO) or accounts receivable term. This is the average length of time for your customers to pay their invoices to your company. This is important because high delinquency of accounts receivable means that your company has limited cash flow to liquidate debt. To compute current DSO at the end of any month, divide current month's sales revenue by thirty (days). Divide that amount into current end-of-month accounts receivable. The answer is the DSO for that month. Example: when sales for September of $860,000 are divided by thirty (days), the answer is $28,667, which is average daily sales divided into accounts receivable for the month of $640,000 amounts to 22.3 equals day sales outstanding (DSO) for September.

Inventory Turns (IT): This ratio is important because it lets you know if your company has obsolete inventory or if your company is maintaining inventories that are too high or too low. When inventories are too high, investment is high, and cash flow is retarded. If inventory is low, shipments to customers may be delayed, and quality may be affected. See Appendix C, Inventory Turns

Important information can also be gleaned from the monthly *profit and loss statement.* Some of these are:

- Productivity (See Chapter 68)
- Breakeven (See Chapter 12)
- Other important percentages include tracking from month to month and year to year the changes in sales revenue, total payroll, direct payroll, materials used, cost of goods sold, gross profit, and net income or net profit (pretax).
- Simply divide the line item for the month or year by total income for the same period yielding a percentage. Chart the changes in these percentages over time to determine what needs "fixing."

Chapter 73

RECYCLING

Recycling is rewarding.

Whether or not you believe in climate change or "green" living or if you have reverence for the "earth," every company should recycle everything possible. It is good business.

In some cases, it can be profitable as well as well as rewarding from an altruistic standpoint.

An amazingly long list of items can be recycled to minimize dumpsites and reduce the need for virgin natural resources such as iron ore (iron and steel), trees (paper), bauxite (alumina/aluminum), and petroleum (hydrocarbons/plastic bottles).

Create habits and a company (and personal) culture of recycling.

Chapter 74

REENGINEERING

Small losses are cumulative and may go unnoticed until the pungent fumes of failure fill your nostrils.

When trends in profits, productivity, safety, attitude (morale), or sales starts spiraling downward, it may be time to go up to the figurative mezzanine of the company and look down at what is going on and realize that changes have to be made. Sometimes the challenge of fixing the leaks in the company hull may be overwhelming. You may feel that the accumulated problems are so great that a lot of time, effort, and money will be required to bring the company back to profitable, viable operating stature.

It may be time to consider reengineering your company. This means reinventing the company culture, the process of individual and group performance, evaluation of products, and services. Reengineering is a renewed focus on quality, productivity, safety, and attitude. Market trends will be analyzed and altered as necessary. Reengineering is the equivalent of taking your car to the garage for a complete overhaul.

You may even need to bring in some outside help (see Chapter 25, Consultants).

If your company is in a descending spiral and needs assistance, don't wait until it is too late

Chapter 75

RELIGION

No one can serve two masters. Matthew 6:24

Many, if not most, U.S. citizens practice religion to some degree. Faith in God provides guiding principles in life. Reading the Bible and religious books and literature often provides a moral compass for people who would otherwise drift through life without some form of spiritual guidance.

On the other hand, there are many people who have a vague interest in religious thought and activity, and there are those who are agnostic or atheist.

However, business and religion only intersect in the manner business is conducted on an honest, ethical basis. A place of business is no place to recruit or solicit employees, customers, or suppliers to adopt and practice your religious beliefs. In general, it is inappropriate to promote any discussion of religious beliefs.

If the founder, owner, general manager, or other company leader is a person of faith, he or she should be expected to operate the business along principles recommended by that faith and beliefs. On the other hand, if company officials are not believers in some religious conviction, business transactions should always be conducted along ethical lines and cultural values.

If employees desire to discuss religion in civil discourse, it need not be discouraged; but owners, managers, or supervisors should never devote any time or energy to interest or coerce employees in any specific or general religious belief.

Chapter 76

RENT

Rent expense is the same whether the space is used one hour or twenty-four hours each day.

Let's say the rent on your building space amounts to $2,000 per month. You are paying rent for the full commercial use of the walls, roof, and floor along with whatever amenities are included such as restrooms, parking and office, storage, warehouse, and display space.

Now let's say that the space is five thousand square feet. Cost per square foot per month amounts to 40¢ per square foot. Because the ceilings are sixteen feet high, you can build a mezzanine or an accessible deck at about nine feet without compromising the space below. If the mezzanine or deck is 8' wide and 60' in length, you have added 480 square feet of storage space. Rental cost of space has now been reduced to 36.5¢ per square foot per month.

If your company is open eight hours each day and an average of twenty-five days per month, the hourly rental is $10 per hour. If operating hours are increased to ten hours each day, rent, a fixed expense, is reduced to $8 per hour per month.

Let's say your company is a bicycle shop where bicycles and other items with wheels are assembled, repaired, and maintained. This work can be done on evenings by a young couple who are bicycle enthusiasts and are able to put in two hours three nights each week. If they work twelve evenings per month, rental costs can now be spread over 274 total hours of operation for a unit cost per hour per month of $7.30.

There are many ways to find thrifty savings.

Chapter 77

RESULTS

Process is important; results are vital.

The company supervisor, manager, or boss that believes in micromanagement for every process and activity in the company is guilty of self-deception and is cheating his company. A supervisor at any level should be spending considerable time planning ahead. While the job of hands-on workers is to produce goods and services, the supervisor's job is to achieve results.

If you are a supervisor, think of yourself as an orchestra director. Your job is not to play all the instruments in the orchestra but to make each musician, through their instrument, contribute their best to the overall music being presented. The result is beautiful music enjoyed by those who are listening as well as those participating. Professional musicians become well known for their results of producing great music.

You can become more valuable as a worker or as a supervisor, manager, or leader when you focus on results. In fact, it is highly probable that production workers, delivery drivers, installers, and computer operators often come up with ideas that improve the process while accelerating and improving the quality of results. Never underestimate the creativity of your workers when you unhook the leash and encourage creative thinking.

Results orientation has several components: (1) finish with planned quality; (2) finish on time; (3) finish on budget (cost); and (4) customer is completely satisfied.

Chapter 78

SAFETY

All accidents are preventable.

Safety is so important that if a new employee has any kind of accident during the first thirty days of employment, it may be a harbinger of things to come. Whether the accident was with a personal or company vehicle, or if the accident was a fall, a serious injury that required time off, consider dismissal without prejudice. Accident-prone employees are expensive.

Frequent but brief safety meetings will help keep safety in the forefront of workers' thoughts. Get your insurance company representative involved and have discussions with workers in all units.

There is a documented case of a filing clerk who tripped over an open file cabinet drawer and was unable to work for more than a month. Accidents can happen anytime anywhere. And they are truly preventable.

See Chapter 1, Accidents.

Chapter 79

SALES MANAGEMENT

Selling requires inspiration, both of self and others; if either prerequisite is lacking, that person should pursue alternative employment.

Sales revenue is truly the key to the pursuit of business excellence. But for best results, all sales must be complete, profitable, and paid for on time by the purchaser. Sales revenue is the core of the business plan. Sales plans as a component of the business plan should be objective and accurate based on facts and wise assumptions.

Sales managers should work with their sales people to create frequent forecasts and compare those projections with actual performance. When sales are greater than planned, the sales person should be congratulated and compensated appropriately. When sales volume is less than plan, the entire company is affected negatively. Thus, sales management must step in and determine what problems exist that must be solved.

The job of sales management is not to seek and relay excuses but to solve problems as they arise to assure that the products and services offered by the company serve the needs of prospects and customers. When company offerings don't coincide with customer demands, all levels of company management must be convened to adjust products, services, prices, quality, and all other aspects of product and service offerings to increase profitable sales.

If changes agreed upon at all levels of company management do not produce positive results in improved sales, it is time to take a hard look at the process for making decisions in the company and the people that make those decisions. See Chapter 53, Marketing.

All business plans start with the sales revenue forecast.

Chapter 80

SECURITY

Trust but verify. –Ronald Reagan

Losses by employee and customer theft cost businesses billions of dollars each year. All companies are vulnerable to losses. Steps can be taken to avoid or at least minimize losses. Think in terms of reducing exposure to risk. The first and most obvious security solution is to install cameras in strategic places. Locations where cash transactions are handled are the most logical places for cameras. Make sure your employees are in the surveillance zone, and customers should be featured as well. Check cameras frequently to confirm that they are working properly; a nonworking camera is worthless. Be sure that employees don't deliberately unplug or in some way assure a malfunction.

Other security measures include mirrors that reveal activity in confined or secluded locations of the facility. These are especially important in retail stores but can also help security in warehouses. If no one looks in the mirror regularly, inappropriate activity can be carried on without being noticed.

There are a host of other measures that can be instituted. For example, if paper invoices are used, make sure each one is accounted for daily. If cash changes hands, make sure a cash register tape is reviewed daily. If your company has inventory, keep it on your computer but also spot check a random list of items each month. Rotate sending people to the bank using different routes and different times daily. Have your auditing firm report anything that looks suspicious in your bookkeeping and accounting records.

If you ship inventory items by truck, be sure that someone signs off at the time of loading and confirm each item with the driver's endorsement. Your receiving people should be trained to sign for each item received and to report irregularities. Leave nothing to chance, and if any activity looks suspicious, investigate.

An important rule is to avoid temptation by gently warning employees and shoppers that active surveillance is present at all times. In virtually every city, town, county, borough and parish law enforcement officers will advise of potential theft risks at your place of business.

Chapter 81

SEGMENTATION

Each business unit should have a planned and actual topline and bottom line for evaluation and control.

Most small businesses have several skill sets to provide different services or products from one location or multiple locations. Let's say that you are a mechanical contractor. If you have plumbers, electricians, HVAC, refrigeration, and gas capabilities, keep records of costs, expenses, and sales for each segment. By so doing, you can determine where to spend money on capital improvements, advertising, and display.

If you are a hardware store, keep records for all the departments such as paint, cabinet hardware, fasteners, and other product departments that produce cost, expense, and profit. A construction remodeler should keep separate records for kitchen remodeling, decks and patios, roofing and window installations.

Another important factor that is valuable in keeping segment records is productivity, the measure of the lifeblood of all organizations regardless of size. In keeping segment records, be sure to record basic cost plus freight in and freight out (logistics), handling and installation labor, inventory turnover, and all costs and expenses. In addition to direct costs and expenses, be sure to record indirect costs of management and administration by segment (or department if you prefer).

In practicing segmentation accounting, it is generally wise to keep profit and loss records on the various functions but create a consolidated balance sheet. If one segment of your business is more (unit) profitable than another, it might be wise to spend more on advertising that segment for example.

Chapter 82

SELLING YOUR BUSINESS

All businesses change hands.

This may be one of the most important undertakings of your life. Selling the business that has been built with capital investment and hard work is a process that must be handled carefully. The expertise of a business broker is often warranted to help achieve the highest value-oriented sale to a qualified buyer in the shortest possible time. Unfortunately, all businesses do *not* sell within the time frame established by the seller.

There are three categories of businesses: those that operate consistently at a profit; those that languish at breakeven; and those that frequently lose money. All businesses may be salable but under different conditions. In addition to profitability, many circumstances determine the transfer or liquidation price (perceived value) of a company. Potential earnings and revenue growth, location, appearance, reputation, competition, financing, demand for services, and condition of inventory and assets are some of the issues that help set the transfer price.

Transfers of business ownership are usually *asset transactions*. If the company is a corporation, the stock is not transferred to the new owners, only the assets. Other organizational structures pass along identified assets, and the liabilities are liquidated by the seller, usually from the proceeds of the sale. Buyers are reticent to incur current or long-term financial liabilities of sellers. In addition, new owners don't want to accept the latent product, service, or personal liabilities that could arise later on. One of the important benefits of an asset purchase for buyers is that they are able to establish new depreciation schedules on assets, reducing taxes, and preserving earnings. It is advantageous for the seller to keep the accounts receivable and dispose of obsolete or unwanted inventory prior to the transfer.

An important rule is: "Always dispose of your business prior to death or disability." The reason is that lawyers, banks, trustees, accountants, and family members usually don't have the time or knowledge to operate a going business even in the short term.

The next rule is: "Your business is worth what an informed buyer is willing to pay a motivated seller at a given point in time." The reason is that the market for businesses, unlike residential real estate, is very narrow and often attracts a limited number of qualified buyers. Businesses that are seasonal in nature are bound to sell better at the beginning of the busy season. Firms that require high investment in equipment and inventory will usually attract a smaller number of interested prospects.

A rule that some business owners fail to observe is: "Sell your business when it is prosperous with a stable workforce and continuing growth potential." Owners who wait until their physical location declines in value, their products or services shrink in demand, and profitability is reduced or disappears. They may be fortunate to realize the discounted market value of their assets.

The process of transferring business ownership is a highly specialized task. Some of the elements involved with this effort are as follows:

1. *Confidentiality.* A high level of secrecy is recommended when your business is being marketed. It is generally preferred that employees, customers, suppliers, competitors, and others don't know of the impending sale of the business. Prospects are always required to sign a confidentiality agreement prior to reading the company profile or financial and operating information.

2. *Communication.* It is imperative that contact is maintained between the seller and the business broker. When prospective buyers make contact, it is often critical that broker and seller need to discuss various aspects of the negotiation. Your office phone, fax, personal phone, e-mail, home and business addresses, beeper, and cell phone information are important.

3. *Financial and Operating Information.* After prospects have signed a confidentiality agreement, they are usually eager to read the company

profile. When buyer's interest persists, financial information is shared with those who appear to be financially and operationally qualified. It is important to provide at least two years of accurate financial data as well as current and historical operating information. Any outstanding commitments to present and/or past customers, suppliers, or employees must be revealed and discussed.

4. *Financing.* Owner financing is sometimes a critical element in making a sale. Buyers may have limited capital but possess other resources that make them qualified. When some owner financing is available, a promissory note (recorded) at current bank interest rates, with a term up to five years with a face value of 50 percent or less of the transaction price is suggested. When the seller can offer some limited financing, capital gains taxes may be deferred, allowing interest-bearing income for a period of time.

5. *Showing the Business.* When prospects are shown the business, first impressions are often lasting ones. It is important that the buildings and vehicles are attractive, the inventory is neat and orderly, and the overall impression is that the business is thriving. When prospects are shown the business during business hours, great discretion is required to retain confidentiality. All showings are cleared with the sellers at least a day in advance.

6. *Marketing.* You know your business better than anyone else. You also know competitors, customers, and others that might be interested in the ownership of your business. Sellers can help develop prospects by providing the names of people or firms that might have an interest in a strategic acquisition or of becoming entrepreneurs. Substantial efforts will be made to advertise and make contact with prospects. Pursuit of a qualified buyer will continue throughout the listing period. Inquiries received by the seller should be promptly forwarded to the business broker.

7. *Negotiations.* The steps in transacting a sale are:

- Developing prospects
- Qualifying buyers
- Showing the business
- Negotiating a sale price and terms
- Execution of an offer to purchase

- Due diligence investigation by buyers
- Producing the transaction documents
- Closing

All these steps take time but will move as quickly as the parties involved are able to make decisions.

Chapter 83

SIMPLICITY

Kiss = Keep it simple, stupid!

Running a business can be made simple or complex. Simplicity is the essence of good business. When giving an explanation, say precisely what is meant in the fewest words possible using understandable words and expressions. When teaching someone how to operate a machine, go carefully through the steps of operation or repair, one step at a time.

Never try to amaze an employee or fellow worker with three syllable words and high-tech phrases.

Simplicity applies to every phase of every business. Simplicity is often repeating the process of the task, whether sales, machine repair, assembly, or handling.

Try to keep all letters and messages to one page; keep signs to as few words as possible to convey the message intended. Keep phone calls brief and to the point.

Simplicity is the spice of life!

Chapter 84

SWOT

Just as you take an annual physical, you should also analyze your business performance each year.

SWOT charts are often used when a new project is being considered or when a new division or a new company is being formed. The term SWOT is the abbreviation for strengths, weaknesses, opportunities, and threats. The four quarters of a chart represented by the four words are obvious. Evaluate the strengths, weaknesses, opportunities, and threats of the company, its products and services compared with the current and future markets as seen by people involved in the operation.

After identifying the company characteristics in each category, add information about how each category can be changed for the better. After the SWOT chart has been completed, assign various individuals or groups to deal with the challenges and report progress in solutions in periodic meetings until you feel comfortable going forward or continuing with the project.

You can develop your own SWOT chart or use some ready-made charts and assistance available from many sources including the Internet.

SWOT	CHART
STRENGTHS	WEAKNESSES
OPPORTUNITIES	THREATS

Chapter 85

TAXES, LICENSES, AND PERMITS

There are three elements of certainty in life: birth, death, and taxes.

Pay taxes on time; it is amazing how fast fees and penalties build up to large sums. If you believe a tax levied on you or your company is incorrect, talk to the appropriate tax people well before the due date. If you don't or can't do that, contact your accountant, enrolled agent, or attorney and try to avoid interminable wrangling that will cost more for professional assistance than the taxes and penalties would have cost.

Explore all possibilities of county, city, and state licenses and permits and keep them current to avoid haggling with local and state officials regarding signage, food safety, handicap access, and other easily overlooked obligations incurred when opening and operating a business.

Government officials and inspectors are usually much more forgiving if business owners establish a modicum of rapport with them in advance of possible or actual violations.

Chapter 86

THEFT

There are a few persons who justify theft by reasoning that the employer is rich and can afford the losses.

One of the greatest tools to prevent or apprehend theft is the security camera. Depending on the size and layout of your business, several cameras located strategically can be monitored in real time or at the end of a day. Theft can be a real squeeze on profits.

If there are rumors or unconfirmed reports floating through your company that someone is converting company products or confidential information such as software, hardware, or documents, it may be worthwhile to obtain the services of a security firm and/or law enforcement.

When a thief (employee or other) is apprehended, it is generally good policy to report the information to the prosecutor and provide all available evidence. In some jurisdictions, prosecutors have little interest in pursuing theft, so regular follow-up is required. Make sure that guilty person(s) is/are prosecuted to the full extent of the law.

Some embezzlements and thefts are so small that it is a waste of time and money to press charges and get involved in litigation. In many cases, getting rid of (employee) perpetrators is the best approach.

See Chapter 80, Security.

Chapter 87

TIME

The common denominator is this: we all have twenty-four hours each day, no more, no less.

We all have exactly the same amount of time in life: twenty-four hours a day, seven days a week. The most successful people are those who use their time most effectively. This does not mean that you must be on the move every minute.

Here is an axiom that has been around forever: plan your work, and work your plan. Don't jump from one unfinished task to another unfinished task. Complete one task and then attack the next one. Make sure priorities are in order of importance and timing. Don't start one task that needs to be completed by Friday while bypassing another task that must be complete by tomorrow.

Make a list of priorities daily. March through each item until completion is achieved. Then follow up to make sure that each activity was handled effectively. There are three steps to each action: *plan, execute, and follow up.*

Time with the company or amount of time in a job should always enhance skills and output. An employee that has been with the company for twelve years should be paid more because of increased efficiency and quality output, not because of twelve years of service.

It is warped thinking that an employee that has worked at the same company for twenty-three years should be retired on the job. The person with twenty-three years' experience should be more productive than workers with less time with the company. People earn paychecks; they don't earn the right to slow down after a certain number of productive years with the company.

Taking accurate inventory is an example of efficient use of time. See Chapter 48, Inventory.

Chapter 88

TRAINING

True story: an untrained worker destroyed $1,200 of merchandise because the machine was unfamiliar to him. Lack of training is expensive.

Here is a rule every company should consider: spend up to 5 percent of each employee's time on training. In a forty-hour week, that is two hours. In a fifty-two-week year, that's about two and a half weeks or about one hundred hours.

What topics or subjects could possibly require two and a half weeks of training each year? Here are some samples:

For construction companies, service firms, and other enterprises where there is moderate to high risk, safety training could be a major contributor to reduced insurance costs, lost time from accidents and even lawsuits. Talk to your insurance carrier; they have experts that teach safety.

For companies that sell services and products, sales and marketing training is always valuable in helping to increase sales. Ethics training is valuable in dealing with customers, suppliers, and employees.

Training of every employee should be an integral part of the employment experience. Perpetual training helps avoid mistakes and errors, saves money.

increase customer loyalty, increase sales revenue, increases employee participation and innovation and contributes to improving morale.

With the speed of changes in technology, culture, travel, communications, and every other facet of personal and business life, constant training is an absolute must. Obsolete equipment and obsolete people create extinct businesses.

Chapter 89

VALUE

Value is measured by the perceptions of customers and prospects.

Value may be defined as a product or service that is equal to or better than other products in the market. Value combines price, quality, fitness for the intended use or application and availability within the time of need by the purchaser.

Remember also that the word *perceived* often accompanies the word *value*. The reason is, of course, that the buyer *always* determines the value of a product or service because it is his/her *perception of quality* that influences the purchase of your products and services.

Here are some of the components of value:

- Communications with employees, customers, suppliers, and stakeholders is always superb. Phone calls are returned immediately, complaints are handled efficiently and quickly, and all other forms of communication are prompt, complete, and totally responsive to the recipient.
- Products and services are completed on time every time. When delays are encountered, revised dates of completion are promptly relayed to customers.
- Employees are friendly and helpful to everyone—no exceptions.
- The place of business looks like a place of business: neat, clean, well maintained.

- Every employee is aware that they are always company representatives by being dressed appropriately on every occasion and being courteous in every situation.
- Value pricing is the company hallmark, not necessarily the lowest or highest price but the price that allows the company to be profitable and always provides the best results for the intended use or application.

Chapter 90

VEHICLES

Never forget that the primary purpose of any vehicle is to get someone and something from point A to point B.

The most important thing to remember about trucks, vans, and cars is that their primary use is to get the driver and whatever else is in the vehicle from one place to another (point A to point B).

For example, you can spend $30,000 on new cars for sales people and give them the thrill of the smell of "newness" and the pleasure of driving a new car. However, that thrill wears off in a couple of days when the aroma of a new car is overridden by the heater or AC, and the driver remembers that his or her job is to simply get them to where they can benefit the company by selling or doing something.

Here's an alternative: buy the same car, a year old, with twenty-five thousand miles on it used at, let's guess, for $18,000. Cars nowadays don't seem to be stressed when they have well over one hundred thousand miles on the odometer. Warning: make sure all periodic maintenance requirements are attended to. Never allow a company vehicle to exceed its normal maintenance guidelines by more than one hundred miles, more or less.

Used vans and trucks can save money too. A truck has an upfront fixed cost, used or new. However, the variable cost of fuel, maintenance, and upkeep can be spread over more miles and greater load values by careful planning. Consider that a van that hauls six hundred pounds of merchandise over three hundred miles per month is less costly to operate per mile than a van that hauls an average of three hundred pounds of merchandise over two hundred twenty miles per month. Plan vehicle utilization carefully.

Every company vehicle should have a daily report of miles, damage, and maintenance (lube and oil change). These records should be filed and monitored for maintenance upkeep.

Appendix A

AMORTIZATION TABLE

Monthly payments required to pay off principal amount of $1,000 at various annual rates of interest (APR) and selected terms from one to thirty years.

PRINCIPAL $1,000								
RATE/Month	0.2708%	0.3333%	0.4167%	0.5000%	0.5833%	0.6667%	0.7500%	0.8333%
RATE APR	3.25%	4.0%	5.0%	6.0%	7.0%	8.0%	9.0%	10.0%
TERM								
Years Months								
1 12	$84.81	$85.15	$85.61	$86.07	$86.53	$86.99	$87.45	$87.91
2 24	$43.09	$43.25	$43.87	$44.32	$44.77	$45.23	$45.68	$46.14
3 36	$29.19	$29.52	$29.97	$30.42	$30.88	$31.34	$31.80	$32.27
4 48	$22.24	$22.58	$23.03	$23.49	$23.95	$34.41	$24.89	$25.36
5 60	$18.08	$18.42	$18.87	$19.33	$19.80	$20.28	$20.76	$21.25
6 72	$15.31	$15.65	$16.10	$16.57	$17.05	$17.53	$18.03	$18.53
7 84	$13.33	$13.67	$14.13	$14.61	$15.09	$15.59	$16.09	$16.60
8 96	$11.84	$12.19	$12.66	$13.14	$13.63	$14.14	$14.05	$15.17
9 108	$10.69	$11.04	$11.52	$12.01	$12.51	$13.02	$13.54	$14.08
10 120	$9.77	$10.12	$10.61	$11.10	$11.61	$12.13	$12.67	$13.22
15 180	$7.03	$7.40	$7.91	$8.44	$8.99	$9.56	$10.14	$10.75
20 240	$5.67	$6.06	$6.60	$7.16	$7.75	$8.36	$9.00	$9.65
25 300	$4.87	$5.28	$5.85	$6.44	$7.07	$7.72	$8.39	$9.09
30 360	$4.35	$4.77	$5.37	$6.00	$6.65	$7.34	$8.05	$8.78

The above table shows monthly payments for selected rates of annual and monthly interest for the principal amount of $1,000.

To find the approximate payments for larger (or smaller) amounts, simply take your subject principal amount and move the decimal point three places to the left and multiply by the appropriate payment in the table.

Example No. 1: A truck is priced at $23,400 with a five-year payment plan at 5 percent. When the decimal is moved three places to the left, the remaining number is 23.4. Multiply this number by $18.87 (from the table) which is equal to $441.56, the approximate monthly payment of principal and interest. You may have to also pay an insurance premium and other costs for other dealer services in addition to the monthly payment. Interest paid will amount to approximately $3,100 over the five years.

Example No. 2: A customer can't pay his bill of $12,361 for purchases he has made from your company. He has asked that you allow him to pay the invoice(s) over a twelve-month (one year) period. Let's say you agree to the one-year promissory note at 8 percent for the full amount. In order to determine the approximate payment, move the decimal three places to the left, and the result is 12.361. Multiply this number by the one-year payment in the table at 8 percent which is $86.99 multiplied by 12.361 which is equal to $1,075.28, the customer's monthly payment for one year. Interest earned will amount to about $542.

Appendix B

CURRENCY CONVERSIONS (INTERNATIONAL)

Because international trade and travel are so commonplace, several countries have been selected to help understand the rates of exchange. The rates of exchange are approximate, and the relationships change daily, so be sure to check the exchange rates prior to trade or travel. Also, note that various agencies and credit card companies offer varying exchange rates.

COL. 1	COL. 2	COL. 3	COL. 4
COUNTRY	CURRENCY	IN U.S. $	PER U.S. $
Canada	Canadian dollar*	.7034	1.4217
China	Yuan**	.1523	6.5666
Euro Area	Euro	1.0861	.9208
Israel	Shekel	.2540	3.9365
Japan	Yen	.008492	117.76
Mexico	Peso	.0559	17.8839
South Africa	Rand	.0596	16.7817
UK (Britain)	Pound (£)	1.4544	.6876

- Note: Data courtesy of *Wall Street Journal,* January12, 2016, page C5.
- Sometimes called the Loonie because of the engraving of the "common loon" on the coin.

**Also called the renminbi.

Examples: When you exchange ONE HUNDRED units of U.S. currency, these will be the results:

COUNTRY	IN US $	PER US $ X Col. 4)
Canada	100 U.S. dollars	142. 17 Canadian dollars$
China	100 U.S. dollars	656.66 Yuan
Euro Area	100 U.S. dollars	92.08 Euros
Israel	100 U.S. dollars	393.65 Shekels
Japan	100 U.S. dollars	11,776 Yen
Mexico	100 U.S. dollars	1,788.39 Pesos
South Africa	100 U.S. dollars	1,678.17 Rand
United Kingdom	100 U.S. dollars	68.76 Pounds (£)

World economies are volatile, and exchange rates change daily.

Appendix C

INVENTORY TURNS

To determine inventory turns, read the notes below this table:

1	2	3	4	5
Month	Inventory	Materials	3/2	12
January	160,000	140,000	0.875	10.500
February	120,000	130,000	1.083	13.000
March	110,000	100,000	0.909	10.909
April	140,000	140,000	1.000	12.000
May	132,000	160,000	1.212	14.545
June	128,000	142,000	1.109	13.313
July	141,000	150,000	1.064	12.766
August	152,000	148,000	0.974	11.684
September	137,000	141,000	1.029	12.350
October	128,000	137,000	1.070	12.844
November	127,000	156,000	1.228	14.740
December	115,000	122,000	1.061	12.730
Total	1,590,000	1,666,000	1.048	12.574

Notes:
Enter month-end inventory in column 2.
Enter material usage for the same month in Column 3.

Divide column 3 by column 2 and enter that amount in column 4.

Multiply the number in column 4 by twelve (months).

The result is annualized number of inventory turns in column 5 for that month.

Using column totals, the inventory turns for the year will appear in the bottom RH cell.

The above table contains fictional numbers and the computations were all done in Microsoft Excel.

Appendix D

MARKUP AND MARGIN

Markup is the percentage of increase over the basic cost plus freight in of merchandise to be resold. From the markup percentage, you need to know the margin each percentage of markup yields so your profit can be planned. Following is a table showing both markup and margin when multiplier in first column is used.

Multiplier X cost + freight-in	Markup % over cost	Margin % on sell price
2.00	100	50
1.75	75	42.9
1.65	65	39.4
1.60	60	37.5
1.50	50	33.3
1.45	45	31
1.40	40	28.6
1.33	33	24.8
1.30	30	23.1
1.28	28	21.9
1.25	25	20
1.20	20	16.7
1.15	15	13
1.10	10	9.1
1.05	5	4.8

In order to establish optimum markup and margin for your company, consider the overall target profit you want to achieve. Using this information, estimate the volume of product sales that will be required by individual product or category. Also, take into account competitive pricing of identical or similar products being offered in your market. Establish a price/volume relationship over time that maximizes profit on each product or product category. Sale prices are governed by product cost, competitive pricing, reputation, services offered, inventory investment, and buyer's perception of value offered by the seller.

Appendix E

LINEAR EQUIVALENTS: FRACTIONS, DECIMALS, METRIC (MM)

Fraction	Decimal	Metric (mm)
1/64	0.016	0.40
1/32	0.031	0.79
3/64	0.047	1.19
1/16	0.063	1.59
5/64	0.078	1.98
3/32	0.094	2.36
7/64	0.109	2.78
1/8	0.125	3.18
9/64	0.141	3.57
5/32	0.156	3.97
11/64	0.172	4.37
3/16	0.188	4.76
13/64	0.203	5.16
7/32	0.219	5.56
15/64	0.234	5.96
1/4	0.250	6.35
17/64	0.266	6.75
9/32	0.281	7.14
19/64	0.297	7.54

Fraction	Decimal	Metric (mm)
33/64	0.516	13.10
17/32	0.531	13.49
35/64	0.547	13.89
9/16	0.563	14.29
37/64	0.578	14.68
19/32	0.594	15.08
39/64	0.609	15.48
5/8	0.625	15.88
41/64	0.641	16.27
21/32	0.656	16.67
43/64	0.672	17.07
11/16	0.688	17.46
45/64	0.703	17.86
23/32	0.719	18.26
47/64	0.734	18.65
3/4	0.750	19.05
49/64	0.766	19.45
25/32	0.781	19.84
51/64	0.797	20.24

5/16	0.313	7.94		13/16	0.813	20.64
21/64	0.328	8.33		53/64	0.828	21.03
11/32	0.344	0.73		27/32	0.844	21.43
23/64	0.359	9.13		55/64	0.859	21.83
3/8	0.375	9.53		7/8	0.875	22.23
25/64	0.391	9.92		57/64	0.891	22.62
13/32	0.406	10.32		29/32	0.906	23.02
27/64	0.422	10.72		59/64	0.922	23.42
7/16	0.438	11.11		15/16	0.938	23.81
29/64	0.453	11.51		61/64	0.963	24.21
15/32	0.469	11.91		31/32	0.969	24.61
31/64	0.484	12.30		63/64	0.984	25.00
1/2	0.500	12.70		1	1.000	25.40

Appendix F

METRIC CONVERSION CHART

FROM METRIC		
APPROXIMATIONS (nonscientific)		
From	Multiply by	To
LENGTH		
millimeters (mm)	0.04	inches (in)
centimeters (cm)	0.4	inches (in)
meters (m)	3.3	feet (ft)
meters (m)	1.1	yards (yd)
kilometers (km)	0.6	miles (mi)
AREA		
Sq. centimeters (cm^2)	0.16	sq. inches (in^2)
sq. meters (m^2)	1.2	sq. yards (yd^2)
sq. kilometers (km^2)	0.4	sq. miles (mi^2)
hectares-10,000 m^2	2.5	acres
WEIGHT (Mass)		
grams (g)	0.035	ounces (oz)
kilograms (kg)	2.2	pounds (lbs)
tonnes-1,000 kg (t)	1.1	short tons (2,000 lbs)
VOLUME		
milliliters (ml)	0.03	fl. ounces (fl. Oz)
liters (L)	2.1	pints (pt)

liters (L)	1.06	quarts (qt)
liters (L)	0.26	gallons (gal)
cubic meters (m³)	35	cubic feet (ft³)
cubic meters (m³)	1.3	cubic yards (yd³)
TEMPERATURE		
Celsius (°C)	9/5(°C)+32	Fahrenheit (°F)
Celsius = Fahrenheit at -40°		

Appendix F

METRIC CONVERSION CHART

TO METRIC		
APPROXIMATIONS (nonscientific)		
From	multiply by	To
LENGTH		
inches (in)	2.54	centimeters (cm)
feet (ft)	30	centimeters (cm)
yards (yd)	0.9	meters (m)
miles (mi)	1.6	kilometers (km)
AREA		
square inches (in^2)	6.5	sq centimeters (cm^2)
square feet (ft^2)	0.09	sq meters (m^2)
square yards (yd^2)	0.8	sq meters (m^2)
square miles (mi^2)	2.6	sq kilometers (km^2)
acres	0.4	hectares (ha)
Weight (Mass)		
ounces (oz)	28	grams (g)
pounds (lb)	0.45	kilograms (kg)
short tons-2,000 lb	0.9	tons (t)
VOLUME		
teaspoons (tsp)	5	milliliters (ml)
tablespoons (tbsp)	15	milliliters (ml)

fluid ounces (fl oz)	30	milliliters (ml)
cups (c)	0.24	liters (l)
pints (pt)	0.47	liters (l)
quarts (qt)	0.95	liters (l)
gallons (gal-US)	3.8	liters (l)
gallons (gal-Can)	4.55	liters (l)
cubic feet (ft^3)	0.03	cubic meters (cm^3)
cubic yards (yd^3)	0.76	cubic meters (cm3)
TEMPERATURE		
Fahrenheit (°F)	5/9(°F-32)	Celsius (°C)
Celsius = Fahrenheit at -40°		

Appendix G

EMPLOYEE REVIEW   Date: _____

Employee's name: _____

Home address: _____

Home phone: _____ Cell phone: _____

Date of employment: _____ Job title: _____

Next of kin: _____ Phone: _____

Supervisor's name: _____

EVALUATION 1 X = Excellent, 5 X = Unsatisfactory

Accuracy in work performance: Supervisor 1. ___ 2___3___4___5___
Employee 1.___ 2___3___4___5___

Ability to follow directions: Supervisor 1.___ 2___3___4___5___
Employee 1.___ 2___3___4___5___

Works with supervisor(s): Supervisor 1.___ 2___3___4___5___
Employee 1.___ 2___3___4___5___

Works with co-workers: Supervisor 1.___ 2___3___4___5___
Employee 1.___ 2___3___4___5___

Arrives/departs on time: Supervisor 1.___ 2___3___4___5___
Employee 1.___ 2___3___4___5___

Creative with time and job: Supervisor 1.___ 2___3___4___5___
Employee 1.___ 2___3___4___5___

Positive attitude: Supervisor 1.___ 2___3___4___5___
Employee 1.___ 2___3___4___5___

Works safely: Supervisor 1.___ 2___3___4___5___
Employee 1.___ 2___3___4___5___

Productivity: Supervisor 1.___ 2___3___4___5___
Employee 1.___ 2___3___4___5___

Quality output: Supervisor 1.___ 2___3___4___5___
Employee 1.___ 2___3___4___5___

Communicates well: Supervisor 1.___ 2___3___4___5___
Employee 1.___ 2___3___4___5___

Overall performance: Supervisor 1.___ 2___3___4___5___
Employee 1.___ 2___3___4___5___

Appendix G

See Reverse Side-------→

History of Past Reviews, Job Changes, Increases/Disciplinary Actions:

Start date: _____ Compensation: _____

Dates and Actions:

_____

_____

_____

_____

_____

_____

_____

Recommended job changes, compensation, actions, effective (date): _____

_____

_____

_____

_____

Individual goals and timetable for achievement: _____

_____

_____

Comments by employee: _____

_____

_____

_____

All the above information has been read by employee, supervisor, and a management representative.

_____   _____

Employee's Signature   Date

_____   _____

Supervisor's Signature   Date

_____   _____

Management Representative   Date

Appendix H

EMPLOYMENT APPLICATION

Name (print): _____

Home Address (street or apartment number) _____

City, state, zip: _____

Birthplace (country, state, city): _____

Date of birth _____

Home phone _____ Cell phone: _____

Social Security Number: _____

Spouse or partner (print name): _____ Phone: _____

Person to call in case of emergency (print name): _____

Phone number: _____

Chronic or acute health disorders/disabilities (list): _____

Last school grade completed: _____

Name and location of last school attended: _____

Last employer: _____

Address: _____

Phone number: _____

Prior employer: _____

Address: _____

Phone number: _____

Prior employer: _____

Address: _____

Phone number: _____

List of references (optional)

Names, phone numbers: _____

_____

Signature of applicant: _____ Date: _____

Postscript

All businesses change hands. There are several reasons for transferring ownership of businesses that have been formed and operated successfully by an enterprising entrepreneur. One signal is when the owner looks forward to the weekend more than Monday morning.

Another warning is when the owner(s) thirst for the seashore or the mountains for rest and retirement. A third and important threat is when illness or some sort of infirmity descends upon the owner(s).

Finally, there may come a time when your dampened spirits think of tax deadlines, debt payments, and the incessant challenges of all aspects of business. When any one or more of these flags goes up, start a strategic plan for the transfer of ownership. In some cases, even many, you may not receive what you think is appropriate compensation. However, when it is time, take the step into the unknown and find release.

The vibrant memories of what you did with your life, the people you influenced, and the value you and your company created will sustain you.

Printed in the United States
By Bookmasters